Teaching
at the
Top of the World

Odette Barr

Pottersfield Press
Lawrencetown Beach, Nova Scotia, Canada

Library and Archives Canada Cataloguing in Publication

Title: Teaching at the top of the world / Odette Barr.
Names: Barr, Odette, 1960- author.
Identifiers: Canadiana (print) 20200172727 | Canadiana (ebook) 20200172743 | ISBN 9781989725030
  (softcover) | ISBN 9781989725047 (HTML)
Subjects: LCSH: Barr, Odette, 1960- | LCSH: Teachers—Grise Fiord (Inuit community)—Biography. | LCSH: Inuit—Education—Grise Fiord (Inuit community) | LCSH: Inuit—Grise Fiord (Inuit community)—Social life and customs. | LCGFT: Autobiographies.
Classification: LCC LA2325.B365 A3 2020 | DDC 371.10092—dc23

Cover photograph: Odette Barr

Back cover image: YoAnne Beausejour Beauchamp

Cover design: Gail LeBlanc

Pottersfield Press gratefully acknowledges the financial support of the Government of Canada for our publishing activities. We also acknowledge the support of the Canada Council for the Arts and the Province of Nova Scotia which has assisted us to develop and promote our creative industries for the benefit of all Nova Scotians.

Pottersfield Press
248 Leslie Road
East Lawrencetown, Nova Scotia, Canada, B2Z 1T4
Website: www.PottersfieldPress.com
To order, phone 1-800-NIMBUS9 (1-800-646-2879) www.nimbus.ns.ca

Printed in Canada

Pottersfield Press is committed to protecting our natural environment. This book is made of material from well-managed FSC®-certified forests and other controlled sources.

For YoAnne,
My kindred spirit

Table of Contents

Prologue

My partner YoAnne and I spent nearly ten years completely immersed in Inuit culture from 1989 to 1999. We left Atlantic Canada to teach in the Baffin region of the Eastern Arctic. This memoir is my account of our arrival and subsequent experiences as teachers and community members in three different Inuit settlements. Although this book offers a glimpse into the everyday life in a remote northern hamlet, specific attention is given to the cycle of the seasons, language and culture, artistic expression, and community input within Inuit schools.

The year 2019 marked twenty years since we left Grise Fiord, the most remote community in the Canadian Arctic, to return home to New Brunswick. While we lived in the North, prior to the creation of the political entity of Nunavut, Inuit already referred to their land as *Nunavut*. Nunavut (meaning *Our Land*), Canada's newest territory, also celebrated its twentieth anniversary in 2019. Much has occurred in Nunavut over those two decades. In some ways, it remains the same place but in other ways, it is now quite different.

The narrative that follows is a snapshot in time documenting my life teaching young Inuit in three different communities throughout the ten years prior to the official birth of Nunavut. It relates the experiences of one person who was a teacher, assistant principal, and then a teaching principal in kindergarten to grade 12 schools in isolated, fly-in communities. It's told from the perspective of a non-Inuit woman, who has worked, lived, and adjusted reasonably well within an Inuit cultural environment. I present Inuit cultural information at many points along the way so that the reader may more completely understand and appreciate the context of the school within its community. I do not pretend to know Inuit culture to any great depth. I can only comment on what I observed, experienced, and learned while living there.

At its core, this memoir is a love story that expresses my great admiration and respect for Inuit people, their culture, and the magnificent Arctic landscape in which they live. I have a unique story to tell. So few Canadians travel to the Arctic, let alone make it their home for a decade. Far fewer write about their experiences there. We were also active members of the three communities, separate to our role as *Ilisaiji* – teacher. The focus is mainly on time spent in Grise Fiord, Canada's most northern permanently inhabited community, located on the south shore of Ellesmere Island. However, I also recollect experiences and memories from both Pangnirtung and Hall Beach, more southerly locales in the Baffin region of the Eastern Arctic. The names of a few people have been changed.

Grise Fiord holds a special place in our hearts. A hamlet of only 150 people at the time, it is spectacularly located on the northern shore of Jones Sound, at the base of a 600-metre mountain. While YoAnne and I lived and taught in Grise Fiord, it was considered by many to be one of the most friendly, peaceful, and beautiful Inuit settlements in Nunavut. Grise Fiord is also one of the High Arctic Exile communities – the history of which very few southern Canadians are aware.

This narrative details numerous cultural activities and events within the school context, and celebrates all people, young and old, of the North. It also reveals the surprises, challenges, and delights facing a southerner who moved to the Arctic. I consider it a great privilege to have had the opportunity to live with Inuit. There is so much that people don't know about this amazing place. In today's climate of truth and reconciliation, I believe that people the world over are ready to open their eyes and hearts to the lives of Indigenous peoples and cultures. This story is for anyone interested in Indigenous cultures (Inuit in particular), and the teaching and education of minority cultural groups anywhere in the world. I was profoundly affected by my experiences in the Arctic. I found I needed to re-examine my beliefs, values, and attitudes with respect to teaching and to life itself.

After reading this memoir, I would hope that readers have a fairly realistic picture of what it was like teaching Inuit students during this particular time in isolated northern communities. I discuss the highs and lows, the successes and challenges, but mostly I reminisce with great fondness about the students and their lives. I hope that readers come to understand that to be a successful northern teacher, you must enter into the lives of your students and their rich culture in very significant ways. I have painted as true a picture as possible, although one completely from my own personal point of reference and experience as a teacher of Inuit students.

1

Ilisaiji! (Il-ee-say-yee)

I pressed my nose against the oval window beside my seat in the Twin Otter. Although we were flying northeastward directly over Jones Sound, thousands of metres in the High Arctic air, the mountains of Ellesmere Island to the north and Devon Island to the south appeared close. I knew they were rugged, but they gave the impression of dreamy smooth slopes – an illusion produced over the great distance between the land and my seat on that small propeller plane. I twisted in my seat to get a better view.

The land below was charcoal gray, striped with dark, vertical trenches and spotted with patches of brilliant white. Flat-topped mountains nearest the varied shorelines sported deep crevasses that plunged to the sea. Cliffs reached upwards on both sides of the sound. Here and there, a long finger of the sea cut into the mass of rock, forming a fiord that stretched out of view. From our vantage, the ultramarine water punctuated with bright white polygons of floating ice hinted at mosaic pieces waiting to be maneuvered into place. Sometimes the ice was so tightly packed, very little blue showed through; other times just a few white specks dotted the cobalt expanse of sea.

Lost in my thoughts, I peered down at the bits of ice, trying to appreciate the scale of the landscape. *Were those chunks as small as a house or as big as a football field?* Impossible to tell. *Was that a polar bear?* I scanned with great hope. *From this altitude, would I be able to see a pod of beluga whales swimming under the surface?* Every chunk of ice became a possible bear or whale.

The weather was perfect, an unusual occurrence for that time of the season, we would soon learn. No clouds, only the cerulean sky. Except for the plane's wings, propellers, and wheels, and the dirt clinging to the exterior of the windows, not much obscured that open sky. The clear air amplified the already sharply defined landscape. The loud droning of the twin engines confined all of us to our inner thoughts. Periodic bubbles of excitement rose to the surface. *Pinch me. We are flying to our new home ... in a propeller plane!*

My partner, YoAnne, sat beside me, quietly taking in the glorious sights through the small windows. We were on our way to teach in an isolated Inuit community on the south shore of Ellesmere Island in the High Arctic. We weren't worried in the least that we were a same-sex couple moving into a remote, fly-in community. We had been up front about our relationship when we were interviewed by phone at our previous teaching assignment. We had told Larry, the chairperson of the Grise Fiord Education Council, that we were a couple. We asked if he thought this would make anyone in the community uncomfortable, and if so, we would understand and simply go elsewhere. Larry didn't hesitate at all. "No, no, that is no problem."

In all the years we had spent in the Arctic prior to travelling to Grise Fiord, we had never experienced one bit of trouble from Inuit with respect to our relationship. We always found Inuit to be respectful, non-judgemental, accepting people. We experienced nothing but warmth and welcome. Each time we moved to a different community though, we felt the need to "feel the waters" and be completely open with people right away. We did not want to find ourselves in difficult situations in remote communities with no chance of being able to leave at a moment's notice, if necessary. As it turned out, we never had to worry at all.

Only two other passengers were with us on the flight from Resolute Bay, the last leg of our trip, on that mid-August day in 1995. Two Inuit men were returning home – a young, tanned hunter with a broad white smile, and a stocky elder wearing a wool cap and thick, dark-rimmed glasses. It had been a long day of travel already. We had left Moncton, New Brunswick, at seven o'clock in the morning, heading west to Ottawa. After an hour's wait, and a change of airline, we flew another three hours north to Iqaluit, on the south end of Baffin Island. We waited and changed planes again before continuing on for the two-hour trip north to the mining community of Nanisivik, just east of Arctic Bay. There, we had picked up a few more passengers and flown northwest to Resolute Bay on Cornwallis Island.

YoAnne and I were accompanied by Figgy Duff, a Newfoundland-Chow mix, who spent most of the time napping in his kennel on the floor by our feet. Packed tightly around his crate were haphazard boxed cargo and bits of luggage, strapped in place in the front section of the plane, directly between us and the cockpit. We worried that Figgy might not make each successive connection with us. Thankfully, he did.

We worried about other things too. Had all of our personal effects arrived in our new home, or would we have to wait for weeks before seeing our clothes, books, music and everything else of importance to us? We had brought enough gear in our luggage to live with for a few weeks, just in case. At least we knew the ropes as we had taught in two other Baffin settlements over the previous six years. We had a good idea of what to expect, but one of the accepted tenets of living in the Arctic is to expect the unexpected, to plan for everything possible.

We had packed a frying pan, a saucepan, a coffee pot, and lots of packaged soup, juice and rice. We knew we would be able to buy a few food items at the local store but variety would be limited. And could we afford it long term? Northern food prices are shocking. Regardless, we would not starve. We had enough clothes with us to last two or three weeks if need be. We had waited six weeks for personal effects to arrive in Pangnirtung in the late 1980s and prayed we would not have to endure that again. It is difficult enough moving to a completely new environment and having some precious personal belongings with you provides immeasurable comfort. We had packed up our things in June and were optimistic in hoping that two months was enough time for our belongings to arrive in Grise Fiord. But we still worried.

The one item we desperately needed to arrive, more than anything else, was our chest freezer. If the annual sealift ship carrying our frozen, dried and canned goods for the next ten months cruised into the community before our freezer did, we'd be in a predicament. Where would we put all our meat, vegetables, and frozen juice, not to mention the chocolate eclairs and other treats to help get us through the cold, dark winter? We crossed our fingers.

Having made similar August trips into the Arctic several times before to other communities, YoAnne and I felt like old hands at travelling north each summer. Heading to Grise Fiord was different – it held a special allure. The name comes from the Norwegian word *grise*, meaning "pig." At the turn of the nineteenth century, the explorer, Otto Sverdrup, thought the grunting sounds made by the numerous walrus in the area reminded him of pigs. In Inuktitut, the language of the Inuit, Grise Fiord is known as *Ausuittuq*, meaning "land that never thaws." It is one of the northernmost communities in the world, situated at nearly 77 degrees north latitude, only 1,500 kilometres from the North Pole.

Many are curious about this small, remote Inuit hamlet, yet very few ever get the chance to see it firsthand. YoAnne and I were thrilled. We both loved the North, its land and its people. And now, we had the opportunity to live and teach in Grise Fiord. It was a dream come true. We had turned down the opportunity to teach here six years earlier, opting instead to go to Attagoyuk School in Pangnirtung, much further south on Baffin Island. "Pang," or Panniqtuuq, meaning "place of bull caribou," is a much larger community with a bigger school and many more teachers for collegial support – an important factor to consider for that first critical year of teaching in a remote Arctic settlement. To be able to finally work at the school in Grise Fiord was something neither of us was willing to pass up. We felt privileged.

The previous year, in 1994, we had been at Arnaqjuaq School in Hall Beach, on the Melville Peninsula. Hall Beach, or *Sanirajak*, meaning "shoreline," sat on the western shore of Foxe Basin, north of Hudson Bay. It was less than half the size of Pang, with a smaller school population. YoAnne was the program support teacher, an in-school consultant of sorts, and I was the assistant principal, who also taught all subjects to a split grade 10/11 class. Hall Beach was a community with great needs, but we enjoyed the place very much. People were warm and welcoming. While being questioned by phone for teaching positions in Hall Beach, we announced our relationship early on in the conversation with the two Inuit women conducting the interview. A mere three seconds of silence ended with Goretti, the principal, simply asking, "Can you teach?" We laughed aloud and I quickly responded, "Yes, very well in fact." And that was all there was to that.

Although Hall Beach was a challenging teaching assignment, we felt connected to the students and had intended to stay for at least another year. However, late in the winter months, we caught wind of the need for teachers in Grise Fiord. The most remote, northern school in North America was beginning a senior secondary program and the school board needed someone to teach all subjects to their first-ever high school class. There was no doubt in my mind. I had to be that person. And as luck would have it, the junior high class, a multi-level group of grades 6 through 9 students, also required a teacher. Fate conspired to send YoAnne and I further north the following year.

Early in the afternoon the jet had landed in Qausuituuq, "place with no dawn" – Resolute Bay to southerners. We had a couple of hours to wait before boarding the red and white Kenn Borek Air Twin Otter, which would take us further north still, to Grise Fiord. We took advantage of the time to stretch our legs and walk

Figgy Duff outside the small airport terminal building. Those few hours in Resolute helped us ready ourselves for the last leg of the trip. The air was crisp yet no snow was to be seen. The land was stark and bare, nothing underfoot but rock and gravel. No vegetation was in evidence within sight of the airport.

The handful of people we met were friendly, and those in the know were more than willing to share their limited knowledge of Grise Fiord. Someone inside the airport directed us to a poster tacked on the wall near the luggage belt. The poster showed a silhouetted mountain against a midnight blue sky with a few scattered, lit-from-within buildings in the foreground. Grise Fiord, apparently, at noon in January. The man was dumbfounded as to why we were moving there. Gazing at that poster in absolute wonder, YoAnne and I thought it simply beautiful and we were even more anxious to arrive in our newly adopted home. Another man behind the counter told us the weather was co-operating and the flight would be taking off on schedule. As we boarded the plane, we knew that in one and a half hours we would be home. We thought of Grise Fiord as home even before we arrived. We sensed we would be happy.

The first half of the flight from Resolute Bay takes passengers over the southeast corner of Cornwallis Island before crossing the channel to Devon Island. On those days when visibility is excellent, the ice cap that covers a good section of Devon Island resembles a thick layer of white frosting covering the undulating topography beneath. There are no communities on Devon Island yet Inuit frequently travel there to hunt and fish. As the flight path of the Twin Otter crosses the island, and continues farther eastward, you find yourself looking down at Jones Sound, the body of water separating Devon and Ellesmere islands.

The young man sitting behind me in the plane spoke English quite well and volunteered much information over my shoulder throughout the trip. We had grown accustomed to the sound of the engine but still had to shout to be heard. Oolootie worked as an outfitter, mainly in the spring, and knew the land well. The closer we got to Grise, as locals refer to the hamlet, the more animated his comments became. He pointed here and there, naming bits of land and water for our benefit. In winter, he had snowmobiled back and forth between home and Resolute Bay many times – a 400-kilometre trip, each way. It is still remarkable to me that hunters travel hundreds of kilometres by snowmobile without a map. Oolootie pointed down through the window at a tiny speck of white in the blue azure. *A boat*, he said. The wake behind the tiny craft was miniscule against the vast sea. I thought what keen vision he must have to see small objects in this wide-open space. I would have missed the boat altogether.

As we neared our destination, the Elder at the back of the plane began speaking. He had been quiet most of the way, but we knew he was listening. He would smile at us periodically when our eyes met. With Oolootie's assistance, much of what he said was interpreted for us. The Elder had been at the funeral of a dear friend in Resolute Bay and was glad to be heading home. Pijamini understood a lot of English but struggled when attempting to speak it. He pointed out various landmarks, identifying them with their Inuktitut names. Unbeknownst to us, Pijamini was a cultural instructor at our new school. It was fitting that he was one of our first introductions to the people of the community.

I stole a glance at the view ahead, through the cockpit window. I eagerly awaited seeing the town appear in the distance. The pilot had begun our descent thirty minutes earlier and we were flying much lower over the water. The mountain peaks on the Ellesmere shore were now at eye level. The engines had quieted, but still it was taking forever to arrive. The sea was a mirror all around. Massive ice cakes floated silently on the water's surface.

Pijamini spotted the town first. He pointed through the left-side windows of the plane and I scuttled over at once. The community was far off in the distance, against a stunning backdrop of steep-sided mountains. There were very few buildings. The town appeared insignificant on the landscape. As the plane continued its descent, Oolootie pointed out Greenlander, an imposing 500-metre mountain at the eastern entrance of the fiord near the hamlet. Pack ice had already begun to form on the bay in front of the community. The plane travelled closer and closer toward the mountain behind the tiny collection of buildings.

Just as I was beginning to wonder when exactly we would turn away from the solid rock face of the mountain, the Twin Otter banked sharply left. Its engines roared, upsetting the dog, who until now had been perfectly calm and quiet. We assured Figgy as best we could. Through our right-side windows, all we could see was the gray rock face, patched with bright yellow lichens. We were so close, had the windows been open, I imagined being able to touch bare rock with my hand. Peering down through the windows on the left side of the plane, we could see the town below. A large pinkish building near a small pond dominated its centre; a domed, mustard-coloured structure sat at the back end of town; what I guessed was the school and gymnasium hugged the shoreline; and scattered about were many small houses. Before we knew it, the rough gravel airstrip was visible through the cockpit window directly ahead. The wheels bumped twice, then we cruised down the rock runway.

People of all ages were gathered at the start of the landing strip. There was no terminal building in Grise Fiord while we lived there, so everyone stood outside in whatever weather presented itself as they waited for the plane to arrive. There was always a crowd, especially at the end of the summer when the new teachers arrive. All schools have local Inuit staff as well as the southerners who return or are hired each year, but the arrival of the teachers on the plane always signals the start of the new school year. This particular year, Umimmak School was beginning a senior high school program – this alone was cause for celebration.

As the propeller plane came to a stop, people swarmed in, eager to see who was arriving. I released Figgy from his crate and attached a short leash to his collar. Experience taught me to keep a tight rein on our pet. We were ready to let people get to know our dog before letting him run free for walks on the outskirts of town. We could hear the cheerful chatter of people outside even before the co-pilot left the cockpit to open the side door. Pijamini descended the ladder steps first and was greeted with hugs and handshakes. Oolootie was next, followed by YoAnne, then me with the dog. There was an air of excitement as we took that last step off the plane. Smiling from ear to ear, we looked around at everyone, and everyone looked at us. We inhaled the cool sharp air deeply. Here we were on a plateau between the mountain cliffs and the sea, at the very top of the world. At last.

YoAnne ventured into the crowd. Some brave young children edged closer and closer to me and Figgy. Luckily, he was a gentle soul and allowed the children to stroke his soft black fur. Soon more tentative children dared pet him. The adults then came to shake our hands. Over the years, I have never tired of this ritual at the airstrip. No matter who steps off the plane, even after a short time away, everyone shakes your hand to welcome you home.

"*Ilisaiji*? Are you the new teachers?" we were asked repeatedly.

"Yes! *Ilisaiji!*" we echoed back with enthusiasm. "What's your name?"

Off in the distance, several older students caught my attention. They walked near the perimeter of the group corralling us toward the village's Suburban van. These teenagers appeared more shy and reserved than did the younger children who had approached us earlier. I thought to myself, *These must be my students – the new high school class.* I smiled at them through the crowd.

YoAnne and I were introduced to so many people that day at the airstrip, all of whom we came to know very well over the next four years. Each year after, we would arrive in the third week of August with a thin layer of snow covering the land, or at least a dusting of white on the nearby mountainside. One year there was enough snow on the ground to allow snowmobiles at the airstrip upon our arrival. Regardless of the weather, we were always greeted warmly by many children and community members. What a wonderful way to begin a new school year.

2

Smile Until Your Face Hurts

YoAnne was helped into the Suburban with all of our luggage and I set off walking down the gravel road into town. Figgy needed a walk after his very sedentary day. I kept him close on a short leash. The pink building in the middle of town was our destination – the structure I had seen so clearly from the air just moments ago. It was only a five-minute walk but it felt wonderful to stretch my legs too and to breathe cool fresh air. There is a certain quality to Arctic air that is hard to describe – it starts out as a cool, subtle fragrance then morphs into a rich, exhilarating sensation. I recognize this same feeling once in a while during winter along the coast in New Brunswick, and I am immediately transported back to the North in that moment as I inhale the memory.

A number of children followed me down along the road, being cautious around the dog, yet curious all the same. We chatted back and forth, but for the most part, we just walked and smiled at one another.

Because of a housing shortage for teachers in the community, we were to begin our stay in Grise Fiord living in an apartment at the Health Centre, the pink building near the pond. It was supposed to be available to itinerant health care specialists who visited the settlement from time to time – a doctor, dentist, psychologist, or perhaps a substitute nurse for when the village's one and only nurse went on a well-deserved holiday. Some sort of an arrangement had been made between the Baffin Divisional School Board and Health Board so that YoAnne and I could have a place to live. Housing shortages for both Inuit and non-Inuit exist in nearly every northern community – Grise is certainly not the exception. We were quite pleased with our living arrangements. The school was visible from our south-facing window, just a two-minute walk around the edge of the pond to its front steps; the Co-operative store, that mustard-coloured building we had spotted as we landed, was directly across the road, behind us. The store also housed the all-important post office, our link to the rest of the world. It was perfect.

Although not privy to the wheeling and dealing that must have gone on to procure the Health Centre apartment for us, I am sure this unique arrangement was made possible because the community was about to begin its first ever high school program. Due to its isolation and small size, Grise Fiord was one of the last communities in the Baffin region to have a senior secondary component added to the school program. Community high schools were still relatively new to the Baffin at the time of my arrival in Pangnirtung in the late 1980s. The Department of Education had committed to providing each community, regardless of size, the opportunity to offer a full kindergarten through grade 12 program. It was hoped that community high schools would help to reduce the problem of lower than average graduation rates of northern students. Before community high schools were developed, most young Inuit had to leave their homes to attend a school in a faraway place – usually Iqaluit or sometimes Yellowknife. Most students simply did not go. Many of those who did venture off became terribly homesick and dropped out within a few weeks of the school year beginning.

Students in Grise Fiord, for the most part, did not continue in school after grade 9. Many parents of my soon-to-be students were of the residential schools' generation, where children were forcibly removed from their families and taken away to southern schools for months and years at a time. When I arrived in Grise in 1995, there was only one student attending high school, in Pond Inlet, Mittimatlalik, 450 kilometres as the raven flies on the north end of Baffin Island. Anyone else in town of high school age was either working at one of the few jobs available to them within the community or they were waiting for grade 10 to begin so they could continue their education without having to leave home.

In the south, we take education for granted, in the sense that there is never any question as to whether or not children go to high school within a walk or bus ride from home. I am sure I was not emotionally ready to leave home at the age of fourteen or fifteen. To me, it seems unreasonable to expect young people to leave the comfort and safety of their families and community to gain an education. I cannot imagine the horrors of the residential school system that took five-year-olds away from their families and communities. In light of this history, the addition of the high school program was truly a momentous occasion for the people of Grise Fiord. As an educator, I was very proud to help start a grade 10 program in this remote Arctic community. Both YoAnne and I considered it an absolute privilege to be there.

When I turned the corner with the dog, YoAnne was already at the foot of the steps of the apartment with all of our bags beside her on the gravel. The children who had been walking with me said their goodbyes and immediately ran across the road to the store. Ame, the driver of the van, picked up a couple of suitcases and began mounting the long, steep, metal steps to our apartment door at the side of the Health Centre building. Ame went about his business quietly. Over the years, we learned to expect this quietness from Inuit. People speak to you when they know you and only then when there is something worthwhile to say. Energy is not wasted on idle chatter.

Ame waited for us to open our door with the key we had been given earlier and he stepped into a small hallway jam-packed with cardboard boxes of all sizes. He smiled ever so slightly and remarked in a matter-of-fact tone that he had "brought lots of boxes up these stairs in the last couple of weeks." Apparently, our personal effects were streaming in regularly with each weekly flight from Resolute Bay. Needless to say, we were relieved that some of our personal belongings were already with us. Life was good indeed. After a couple of trips up the stairs and a thank you to Ame, we closed the door of our new home behind us and instantly went about checking to see which boxes had arrived and which were still to come.

The sealift ship was expected in two weeks or so. Besides all of the town's supplies for the upcoming year, the annual sealift brought grocery orders and various other items for individuals. The fact that our freezer had yet to arrive by plane with our personal effects did not really worry us too much. After seeing so many of our boxes in the apartment, we felt assured it would come before the ship arrived with the bulk of our year's groceries. Each year in May we'd receive an updated list of all the canned and boxed food we could order from a supermarket in Montreal. Frozen goods were ordered separately. Community orders were packed in crates on pallets or in freezer containers and put aboard freighters in the port of Montreal. Ships leave in early summer and generally arrive at the various Eastern Arctic settlements anytime in September. In Pangnirtung, Hall Beach, and Grise Fiord, the ship always arrived around Labour Day.

We got fairly good at ordering just the right amounts of the various food items we appreciated having with us throughout the school year. We ordered enough food for ten months at a time. Although we could buy some staples during the year from the local Co-op store, most people, southerners in particular, made huge sealift orders. Many Inuit had begun to place grocery orders through the sealift service as well.

The catch was, however, that not all could afford it as you had to pay upfront for the goods before the ship left Montreal. Even back then, we had to fork out $3,000 or more for that one grocery bill. Our first order, before leaving for Pangnirtung in 1989, took us a full two weeks to figure out. Seriously. How many people know how many kilos of chicken they eat in ten months? How many cans of corn niblets or boxes of cookies does one person consume in a year? Since we were told that bread was expensive (*if* you could find a loaf), we had to determine individual amounts of all of the ingredients needed to make our own bread each year. We couldn't buy single cans or boxes of food from the Montreal supermarket that offered the sealift service, only full or half-cases. To educate ourselves in the fine art of grocery shopping, sealift-style, we'd trudge off to the Superstore in Moncton and take note of how many meals ten kilograms of chicken could make, then estimate how much chicken we wanted to eat and order accordingly. We did the same for pork chops, hamburger and fish. Likewise, we needed to estimate how much pasta and tomato sauce ingredients we'd want, then frozen french fries, fruit juice, soda water ... the list was endless.

I remember a colleague in Pangnirtung commenting that in her first year she mistakenly ordered enough bran flakes to insulate a small bungalow. Yes, many, often humourous, errors were made. We grossly underestimated our toilet paper needs and ran out before the end of our first February. You'd think that toilet paper would be one item always stocked in local stores, but that was not the case in our experience. Quickly organized sealift exchange parties in February or March of each year allowed all of us to even out our supplies to take us to June. One year we ordered far too many cases of tomato paste, but we happily traded the extra cans for other items we needed.

Items for which we needed less than a full case were purchased separately throughout our summer holiday, then either packed with our personal belongings on the plane or mailed north through Canada Post. You can imagine the looks at the checkout aisle in Walmart as YoAnne and I unloaded nothing but ten-months' worth of feminine hygiene products for each of us. Carefully wrapped bottles of soya sauce, ketchup, dried figs, grapefruits, and Twizzlers black licorice made the trip each year wedged safely between pieces of clothing in our luggage.

When each boxed palette of dry and canned items and the

caseloads of frozen goods arrived at our Arctic home, we always felt we'd ordered far too much – but that sentiment soon passed. It was always better to have more than needed. Just in case. We breathed a sigh of relief after every one of our purchases was checked off our list and confirmed to have arrived. Each community has sealift disaster stories where palettes have made the journey all the way past the Arctic Circle only to slide off the barge into the sea as it is tugged from the ship offshore to the beach.

It has been more than twenty years since our last sealift order. To this day, neither of us can stomach instant potatoes, frozen liquid egg whites or powdered milk. Ten years of limited fresh food teaches you to appreciate the cornucopia of richness available in southern grocery stores, even in mid-winter.

At any rate, on that first day in Grise Fiord, although we were extremely tired, we were far too excited to relax and rest. We wanted to take in as much as we possibly could before collapsing with exhaustion on our first night in the High Arctic. As it was not yet the end of August, it did not get dark at night so it was possible to putter around for hours and still be able to glance at the goings-on in the streets outside our apartment windows. During the light period of the year, even very young children can be seen playing on the roads late into the wee hours of the morning. With the pond outside our front window, we often watched kids happily playing with wooden boats at the water's edge.

Our apartment was much nicer than we had expected. It was a two-bedroom, open living space, with a loft accessible by one of those drop-down folding ladders in the hall ceiling. From the loft I could lean over a short railing and look down into both the living room and kitchen. I chose the loft as my personal workspace. I would eventually set up my work table and all of my art materials, including the easel I carried around with me wherever I went. The artist in me couldn't help but feel inspired in this natural studio with a most spectacular view. Over the roof of the school, viewed through our apartment windows, we could see the smooth-as-glass waters of Jones Sound, framed on either shore by the soaring mountains of south Ellesmere Island and the snow-covered peaks of Devon Island off to the south. I cannot recall how late we stayed up that first night, but I am sure we must have done a fair bit of unpacking before collapsing with fatigue. We estimated about half of our belongings had arrived. Ame would have quite a few more trips up those steps yet.

The following day, we explored the community, walked the dog, and met people. I remember moving to Pangnirtung, six years earlier, and to Hall Beach, the previous year, and doing exactly the same thing – walking about town and smiling until our faces hurt. It is so important to get out into the community and meet people. We were not expected to talk to everyone we met but we were expected to nod and smile a lot and to explore every nook and cranny of the community. If I could offer one piece of advice to a newcomer to the North, it would be to simply keep quiet and observe as much as possible. There is so much to see and to learn from the moment you step off the plane. Most Inuit respect people who can quietly observe and take in their surroundings without talking all the time. I learned this over the years and I became quite good at not always filling the silence. It is most definitely an acquired talent for me as keeping quiet over long periods doesn't come naturally.

As we wandered about town, children ran to greet us again. Some we recognized from the airstrip, some we didn't. Cries of *Ilisaiji! Ilisaiji!* reached us from all directions. We knew it was important for us, especially in such a small community, to remember faces as quickly as possible so we could start learning their associated names. Inuktitut names and their proper pronunciations challenge southerners at the best of times. At least we had the benefit of living in two other communities – we knew the Kilabuks, Akpalialuks, and Metuqs in Pangnirtung, and the Curleys, Akearoks, and Irqittuqs in Hall Beach. We would soon be familiar with the Pijaminis, Akeeagoks, and Kiguktaks of Grise Fiord.

As a new teacher, I always made a point to learn my students' names within a day or two. I would ask for help in the pronunciation if needed and then simply risk it. Students love to hear their teachers trying to speak Inuktitut and making funny mistakes.

Most of all, they appreciate being called by their proper names. It seems to me that a large part of effective teaching anywhere involves attention to small but important details, like learning how to pronounce new names quickly.

So YoAnne and I set out on that first full day in our new community to meet people and to get our bearings. We wanted to find out where all of the important places were and how to find anything we needed. For a small hamlet of roughly 150 people, there was still a lot to discover. We walked many kilometres back and forth along the sand and pebbled shoreline, up and down the gravel streets, and across the boulder-strewn plateau between the town and the base of the mountains. There may have been forty or so houses in town as well as several municipal buildings spread throughout the community.

The Grise Fiord Inuit Co-operative, referred to simply as the Co-op, was the only store in town and served as the social centre of the community. If you are looking for someone who you know is in town, but not at home, the first place you go to is the Co-op. The building was a dome-roofed metal structure near the back end of town, next to the large oil and gas silos. Inside, it resembled a typical general store and offered the same types of goods found in any small convenience shop. The startling difference was the price of the items lining the shelves and the fact that a number of the canned goods had expiry dates long past. I recall one Christmas, treating ourselves to a small bag of real potatoes – normally we ate instant potatoes, brought in with our sealift food order. At over one dollar per small potato, we relished each and every morsel!

The Co-op also served as the local agent for Kenn Borek Air and met each plane at the airstrip as it arrived, usually to pick up valuable food supplies that had been airlifted in from Ottawa, Montreal or Yellowknife. Not all food arrived in town on the sealift in September as supplies trickled in with each weekly flight from Resolute Bay as well, but airlifted food cost a lot more.

The Co-op operated a rustic lodge for the various, albeit infrequent, government employees and business people who travelled to town regularly, as well as for the visitors in the growing sport hunting and ecotourism sectors. This two-storey, pale yellow, box-shaped hotel sat on the shore road next to the community gymnasium. Locals could often be seen through the windows of the dining area, sitting at a table chatting with someone over coffee. Located on the edge of a rugged, mountainous island, overlooking an expansive deep-water sound, and facing the glaciers of another far-off island, I would wager that the Grise Fiord Lodge has one of the best views in all of the Arctic.

Situated between the Co-op and the pond was the Health Centre. It was constructed in the early 1990s and is quite a handsome building. Aside from the unusual yet oddly pleasing pink colour, it is what I consider an architectural gift to the community. Unlike the many box-like buildings that dotted most northern settlements at that time, the Grise Fiord Heath Centre had character. There were two wings – one short and one long – on either side of a many-windowed circular boardroom. It was airy and bright and very comfortable for the residents to visit. There was a nurse-in-charge, a local community health representative, and various support staff who took care of the health needs of the community. Cathy, the nurse-in-charge, was also our neighbour as our apartments shared a common wall. Next to the Heath Centre sat a dilapidated trailer, with various add-ons, that housed the Iviq Hunters and Trappers Organization, the Government Liaison and Renewable Resources offices and, at that time, the Nunavut Arctic College office. This trailer was what remained of the original Grise Fiord health centre.

Next door to the Co-op was the relatively new gray and red trimmed Hamlet building. The elected mayor and council made all municipal decisions here, in the small boardroom at the back. Various offices were scattered throughout the "Hamlet," as the building itself was generally referred, including the small room that acted as the community FM radio station. The Canadian Broadcasting Corporation (CBC) allowed communities to broadcast over its airspace on a regular basis. These community radio broadcasts were tuned in to by all, young and old. Every single piece of community information was passed on via the local airwaves.

Kenn Borek's flight from Resolute is delayed again due to the blizzard.

Hannah, please call your mother at home.

Be careful near the dump – polar bears are hanging around the dog ties.

Everyone come to Jimmy's for birthday cake and ice cream.

Of course, everyone listening knew which Jimmy it was. A number of people took turns hosting radio shows at designated times throughout the week. The most popular shows were the call-ins where anyone could speak on air for any number of reasons. And of course, Saturday night radio bingo was a huge success. Don't try to phone anyone at home if the bingo game is on. I must admit, I resisted bingo for three years, but in our final year at the school, both YoAnne and I gave in and played a few games. YoAnne even won one. Well, she thought she had. When she arrived at the station by snowmobile to have her numbers verified, she discovered that she had not understood the rules correctly. They gave her the $50 prize anyway and the entire listening community had a good laugh at the *qallunaaq*, the "white person," who didn't know how to play radio bingo. We both laughed so hard at that incident we wondered why we hadn't played bingo years earlier.

The Hamlet was responsible for all municipal services. Most of the maintenance of the vehicles and machinery took place in the Hamlet garage, in the middle of town, next door to the school. Electricity for light, oil for heat, regular water delivery and septic services, road repair and airstrip maintenance all needed to be kept up year-round. The Housing Association ensured that everyone had a place to live and took care of all of the homes in town, including the constant maintenance of furnaces and water pumps. "Housing" too had a garage and warehouse. The mechanics and maintenance crew of the community are very important people – they keep the hamlet running safely and smoothly. It is sometimes easy to forget how geographically isolated you truly are in a fly-in, Arctic settlement closer to northern Greenland than to anywhere else in your own country.

YoAnne had a sweatshirt with a picture of a saluting polar

bear wearing a red tunic. The logo read "The Grise Fiord RCMP, Canada's Northernmost RCMP Detachment." I smile because every single thing in Grise Fiord is "northernmost." The Royal Canadian Mounted Police detachment was a blue and white trailer halfway between the landing strip and the school, on the gravel road that leads from the airstrip into town. Only one officer policed the entire community, and when vacation time arrived there may or may not have been a replacement sent in. The community had very little crime – the odd occurrence of vandalism, a few break-ins, perhaps one or two alcohol-related incidents. The police officer in Grise Fiord spent a lot of time actively participating in community events. I spent time every Christmas driving around town with both the RCMP officer and the nurse, in the police truck, acting as judges for the annual ice and snow sculpture competition. We were practically the only ones in town without any family affiliations so we were seen to be completely impartial.

A small, plain white structure with a tall spire sat at the bottom of a road, near the east end of town. Two or three nights a week, at seven o'clock, the bell sounded to signify that someone had gone inside to warm up the cold interior by lighting the stove and was ready to greet people at the door. There was no ordained minister for St. Peter's Anglican Church. Aksakjuk, a very quiet man even by Inuit standards, was the lay preacher. He was devout in his dedication to the church and served as the religious leader of the community. When Aksakjuk was not available, Liza, his wife, stepped up or perhaps David or Neevee, or anyone else willing to lead the congregation in prayer. As with most important jobs in the community, there was always someone ready to help out.

YoAnne and I eagerly stepped inside the church on that first tour of the town. We were curious to see what it looked like. We had visited St. Jude's Cathedral, the igloo-shaped dome with a traditional pointed steeple, in Iqaluit and had been impressed with its distinctly northern décor. We were not disappointed with St. Peter's either. The altar was adorned with intricately sewn and patterned sealskins. On the walls around the front of the church were embroidered tapestries depicting traditional Inuit scenes. A narwhal tusk and various ivory and bone artifacts were placed throughout the altar area. Seating in the church was simple – eight or so wooden pews on either side of the aisle. There was a peaceful and comforting feel to the church as soon as you stepped inside. Sadly, St. Peter's burned beyond repair in early 2018. I read in the *Nunatsiaq News* that embers from the wood stove caused the blaze that gutted the church. But knowing the strength of this resilient and tight-knit community, I was not surprised that the church rose again.

As with all northern communities, there are many modern-day conveniences that some southerners may be surprised to see. People's homes look very familiar, as they closely resemble those in the south. Although the vehicles of choice in the North are snowmobiles and all-terrain vehicles, there were a few half-ton trucks parked at various locations in town. While we lived in Grise Fiord, there were no cars at all. Two or three large satellite dishes planted at strategic spots across town told us that telephones and televisions were alive and well in the hamlet. If you called anyone in any northern settlement, you'd notice a small delay or echo in the conversation over the line. This was a result of the "bounce" inherent in the satellite phone system in place. Every now and then, when a blizzard blew into town, the phone dish would get moved or damaged and we'd have to wait for someone to fly in to fix it when the storm subsided. Grise Fiord received cable during our first autumn in town. Every house received free service for a month before deciding whether or not to keep it. I don't think anyone said no after that first month, including us. Every household had at least one television set, sometimes three or four. In fact, my students were surprised to learn that most *qallunaat* teachers had only one television set in their northern homes.

Computer technology had arrived in the High Arctic. However, during our time in Grise, the Internet was only accessible through a gateway in Iqaluit via the school board's electronic bulletin board system. Full-scale e-mail communication to points throughout the world was not yet possible. Nevertheless, the school was very well equipped with Apple computers, printers, digital cameras, and a scanner. All of the town's agencies were networked and some individual families owned personal computers as well. The Hunters and Trappers Organization (HTO) constantly monitored all land travellers near the community with a radio telephone – a high frequency radio. There was at least one portable satellite phone available for emergencies and other situations. Many hunters used a global positioning system (GPS) to aid in navigation, although the old dependable citizens' band, CB, radio was still the standard for communication out on the land.

At any given time, there may have been as many as seven or eight non-Inuit residents in town. All Inuit in Grise Fiord spoke Inuktitut as their first language. Most adults also spoke some English. Very few residents, except for some Elders, were unilingual Inuktitut speakers. Children learned English in school, as well as through watching television. Grise was still very much a traditional Inuit community, in the sense that almost all families relied significantly on food obtained from traditional land activities such as hunting and fishing. This "country food" made up a large proportion of their weekly diet. All families spend a great deal of time throughout the year out on the land. No family is without a *sikidoo* (snowmobile), *qamoutik* (sled), canvas tent, and basic camping gear. Many men in particular hold part-time jobs in the community, which allows them to spend considerable time on the land in various seasons as desired. Part-time employment may include working for the Hamlet, the Housing Association, the Hunters and Trappers Association, the Co-op, the Health Centre, or the school.

As we wandered through town on our first day's exploration, we learned many things. Inuit culture was alive and well in this tiny community. We heard Inuktitut being spoken everywhere we walked. Seal carcasses lay on many front steps. Stretched sealskins on wooden frames sat drying in the sun, strategically placed near the sides of houses or sheds. Walrus heads with full tusks and antlered caribou skulls sat on the tops of plywood shacks. Muskox furs lay about in various stages of drying. Boats tied to large boulders near the shore were being packed or unpacked; many more were already on the waters of the fiord further offshore on Jones Sound. Snowmobiles and sleds sat about uncovered near every house, in wait for the inevitable snow to arrive. A lot of community life looked familiar to our southern sensibilities – small children riding bicycles up and down dirt roads, gleefully aiming for the biggest puddles; people walking and chatting together as they headed into the Co-op or back towards their homes, with arms outstretched carrying heavy plastic bags laden with groceries.

We thoroughly enjoyed discovering our new community on our first day, in August 1995. Of course, at that time we did not know many of the details I have described here. We learned about our community gradually over the coming years. And Grise Fiord did become *home* for all four of those years.

3

The School at the Top of the World

YoAnne and I knew that once we began teaching at the school our time would not really be our own. We'd be so busy planning each day's lessons that we would not likely have time to do a lot of other things. For this reason, we arrived in Grise Fiord nearly two weeks before school started so that we could unpack our things, move in, meet people, and hike a little around the community. After working in Hall Beach and Pangnirtung, we understood and accepted that northern teachers have virtually no time for themselves outside the realm of school. We had arrived a full three weeks before starting school in Pangnirtung, back in 1989, and we wanted to orient ourselves as best we could in Grise Fiord as well. Our routine became one of daily walks around town, exploring the nearby river valley and hiking up the closest hills at the foot of the mountains, and most importantly, chatting to all of the children and adults we met along the way.

Harry, the principal, and his wife, Myrna, had flown in a few days after we had arrived. Harry was returning for a second (and last) year as principal at Umimmak School. I had met him in Rankin Inlet earlier that summer, in July, during my first summer session of the Northwest Territories (NWT) Principal Certification Program. He and Myrna, both from Prince Edward Island originally, had spent three years in Iqaluit, the soon-to-be new capital of Nunavut, prior to coming to Grise Fiord.

We had already met Mimi, the elementary teacher, and Mary, the primary teacher. Both had young families in town – Mimi grew up in Grise Fiord and Mary, originally from Pangnirtung, had married an Inuk from Grise and had lived in the community for several years. We'd also had the chance to meet Geela, the school office manager, and Annie, the custodian. We were told that Abraham Pijamini, the Elder we had met on the flight in from Resolute Bay, often worked as a cultural instructor in the school, as did Rynee Flaherty, Mary's mother-in-law. As it turned out, Geela and Mimi are sisters, and Abraham is their father; Annie is the wife of the then District Education Authority (DEA) chairperson, Larry Audlaluk.

It shouldn't have been surprising to us that there were so many family connections within the school. But it did take us a while to grasp both the significance and implications of living in such a small, isolated community. Pangnirtung had a population of about 1,200 when we lived there, and Hall Beach was about 500 or so. To truly understand what life is like in a community of fewer than 150 people, experience alone gives you a true picture. Harry loved to talk about all of the family connections in Grise. Being from an island, the smallest Canadian province, he already had an appreciation for small town politics. Not surprisingly, family politics became one of many considerations in our school planning over the years. At any rate, by the time school began we felt as if we had been in Grise Fiord much longer than two weeks.

We had met most of the community by this time. The education council had sponsored a community feast to welcome new and returning teachers, and to celebrate the start of the school year. The entire hamlet filed into the gymnasium and after a few short speeches, a prayer, and the traditional lighting of the seal oil lamp, the *qulliq*, we all dug into the incredible amount of food before us. Most community feasts look the same: sheets of plastic and cardboard are placed on the floor, then the raw seal, caribou, and muskox meat are placed at various locations throughout the room. Of course, there is a lot of frozen raw Arctic char as well. Most people still ate a lot of raw meat, but there is always a pot or two of cooked stew on tables in the room. YoAnne and I had grown accustomed to eating some raw meat – we liked all of it, especially the seal meat and the char. Everyone arrived with their *ulus*, traditional Inuit curved knives used for cutting meat while eating (among other things), and their plastic bags for extra "takeout" for home. Elders would always be asked to choose their food first, then the rest of the crowd joined in.

Celebrations in Inuit culture almost always involve the sharing of communal food at a feast. Throughout the school year there would be as many as six to eight community feasts where people gathered to share food and celebrate something or other. New beginnings are always cause for celebration and celebrating is a key component to many northern school programs throughout the year. Not only were we marking the start of a new school year, we were creating the first year of the most northern high school in North America. The entire community was abuzz.

Umimmak School sits on a raised section of gravel between the pond and the dirt road that closely follows the shoreline between the airstrip in the west and the far eastern end of town. *Umimmak* translates as "muskox" and comes from the numerous muskoxen that herd together on the plateaus near the shoreline, not too far from the community. The school building, a tan coloured structure with royal blue metal trim, faces south, with the front steps offering a spectacular view of Jones Sound and Devon Island far off in the distance.

The design of the school is a simple one: a rectangular box with classrooms on the north and east sides, the washrooms, kitchen, office, and various other rooms on the south side. An L-shaped hallway separates the classrooms from the other rooms of the school. There was no school gym but there was an agreement between the Hamlet and the school that allowed students access to the community gymnasium during the day. Students entered the back door of the community gymnasium by exiting the school through a side door and walking across a twelve-metre metal ramp. The school was built in 1991 to replace a terribly rundown structure and had managed to stay in remarkably good condition over the years. The old school could still be seen in two separate pieces along the shore road, near the water. Carefree kids played in the condemned remains of that old building.

The first time I walked into Umimmak School, I was struck by its tidiness and compact use of space. Almost everything needed by a school was there on a very small footprint. I thought how neat and organized everything seemed to be. A glass display case in the front part of the hall highlighted student-made carvings and duffel socks, as well as some locally important artifacts. The bulletin boards were empty, waiting to be filled up once again. The school was the perfect size for a small community. Right away, it felt comfortable to me and I was ready to begin. Schools are very different places without students – unnaturally quiet.

Bright and early on that first day of school, students began filing in through the front doors into the hallway. Everyone was directed to the largest room in the school, my future classroom. About fifty students, aged six to twenty years, found a piece of the floor or a desk and chair to sit at as we all entered the new high school classroom. I had pushed all of the desks, chairs, and tables to the periphery so we could fit everyone in the room. Teachers hurried last minute students from the hall into the classroom and they too joined the crowd.

Some students, we were told, were not yet here because they were still out on the land camping with their families. They would arrive back in town gradually over the next few weeks. This was always to be expected in any Arctic community. The summer season is short enough. If the weather is good into September, people take advantage of it and stay out on the land as long as they can.

Harry, our principal, began with a welcome in English followed by the Inuktitut translation given by Mimi. The new kindergarten students spoke Inuktitut only and most of the primary students still spoke very little English. Every school assembly had to be given in both languages.

Students were very quick to quiet down; after all, they were soon to find out who their classmates were and who their homeroom teachers would be. Of course, many of them already knew these details. In Grise Fiord, if you are in kindergarten, grade 1, 2, or 3 you always have Mary as your teacher; if you are in grade 4, 5, or 6, then Mimi is your teacher. Many of the children YoAnne and I had met had asked which grades each of us would be teaching, so most older students knew which one of us was their teacher. But there were new teachers to be added to the mix. After speaking informally for a while of the notable events during their summer holidays, students were officially introduced to YoAnne and me. Harry offered only minimal information, as we would soon have our students to ourselves in our classrooms for the entire morning. We smiled at the captive group as they listened intently to Harry's and Mimi's every word.

Our objective that morning was to get students into their homerooms as quickly as possible so they could begin to settle into their new surroundings. Harry handed over the floor to the teachers, each with their student list in hand. Children listened carefully for their names. Mary began with her group. It was heartwarming to watch the older grade 1 and 2 students help the new kindergarten students. As each class was called out, the teacher and students would form a single file line at the door and promptly leave my room for their own. Mary's and Mimi's groups had both left. YoAnne called out the names on her list of junior high students, and off went they went next door. The only ones left in the room were my students – this was it, the beginning of the first ever high school program at the top of the world.

In front of me sat seventeen students, the largest group of all the classes in the school. Some had just finished grade 9 the year before; some had been out of school a full year; others had left school two and three years previously. Not all had completed grade 9, but due to their age and number of years out of school they were to continue their education starting with grade 10. I cannot imagine what was going through each of their minds that first day, although I am sure the excitement, nervousness and worry of beginning high school were foremost in their collective thoughts. There was a wide range of ages in the group, from sixteen to twenty, and more boys than girls. Some were already together as boyfriend and girlfriend. One of the girls had a young daughter, who entered kindergarten in our last year at the school.

What beautiful faces! I cannot help but remember those first few days with such warm emotion and happiness – I watched these young people grow and develop into adults. I shared in births and deaths, the joys and sometimes the despair of their lives. None of us in that room knew what the next few years would bring. On that first day in grade 10, however, I needed to share some information about myself, get to know some of the details of their lives, learn a bit about their schooling backgrounds, and give them an indication of what to expect over the next weeks and months. There I was, facing a group of silent and nervous Inuit students. I knew they needed reassuring right away.

"Congratulations!" I exclaimed with a wide smile. "You are the new grade 10 class at Umimmak School."

I explained I was their teacher for most of their subjects and that we would all work together in this classroom each day. I went on to say I had taught high school in Pangnirtung and Hall Beach as well. A few eyebrows lifted, indicating that they seemed pleased to know I had northern experience. I intentionally threw in a few Inuktitut words here and there throughout my introduction, each time eliciting a smile from someone in the crowd. Both YoAnne and I had participated in a three-week Inuktitut immersion course a few years earlier. It was one of the hardest learning experiences of our lives. We learned a lot and developed a good ear for the language but were far from fluent. However, we did manage, at times, to give the appearance that we knew more Inuktitut than we actually did. That alone helped us significantly in the classroom.

I described some of my personal background: I had been a naturalist before becoming a teacher and I had lived in a number of interesting places. I loved the outdoors – camping, hiking, kayaking, skiing – and I especially enjoyed art and music. I tried to give them an idea of what kind of person I was.

The lack of overt reaction to my presentation did not worry me at all. I knew from experience it took time for Inuit students to speak up and participate with new teachers in school. This did not mean they were not paying attention and listening to every single word. I knew they were watching and taking in everything. I have come to understand that Inuit possess highly attuned skills of observation. While in the North, I learned a great deal about the power of silence and of nonverbal communication. Inuit always watch first. I was well aware of this: I understood that the first few days would be quiet. I needed to be patient and calm.

I then began describing the high school program. This is what they really wanted to know most of all. None of them had any high school experience, and most of their parents and older relatives had no experience with schooling above grade 9 either. I explained that many of the courses would be the same as those they were used to, except that a wider variety of subjects would be offered. After describing the expected workload, homework requirements, and the responsibilities of individuals to keep up with the work, I talked about the importance of attendance. My main focus that morning, however, was to convey the idea that becoming a high school student was a remarkable achievement, and they should be very proud to be able to continue their studies in their own community. They could all look forward to graduating with a high school diploma. They were the leaders of the future in Nunavut. This was a big deal.

I described a little about the details of the credit system and the daily routines of high school, about regular tests and exams, but I punctuated my speech with reminders of the special nature of this moment in their lives. These particular students were special – they were the first residents of Grise Fiord to begin high school within the community. Whether they realized it or not, they would become role models for every single student in the school behind them. I wanted to emphasize these facts over and over again. In my mind, they needed to be told it was completely natural to be nervous, but they should also feel great pride in being able to sit in that classroom and to understand they were at the beginning of the next stage of their lives. I often reverted to what became known as the "pep talk" throughout my time at Umimmak School. Educators often forget how difficult it is to be a student. I believe students need to be reminded regularly of their achievements, to consider the "big picture" and to see where they are heading.

Slowly, students began to very quietly ask questions. *How many credits is one course? How many do we need? How many years will it take?* I answered as simply as possible as I did not want to overwhelm them on their first day. Every now and then I would catch one of them looking at a friend, smiling at one another. Sometimes, one or two would explain something to someone in Inuktitut, then patiently look towards me for more information. This was good: they were beginning to get comfortable. I asked about their experiences in school so far, about the kinds of teachers they liked or didn't like in the past, and why they felt that way. But no names please! I explained I liked to be outside a lot and would try whenever possible to have classes outdoors. This generated wide smiles and chatter. I hastened to add we did need to do a lot of regular "reading and writing" work in school but we would take any opportunity we could to cover some of that work outside. Students nodded their heads approvingly.

The most significant words I had to say that first morning was that I promised to stay with them until the first students graduated with a high school certificate. The room fell silent for several long seconds before one brave soul inquired, "What if it takes a long time?"

I replied I was sure that some of them could finish in three or four years. Without realizing it I had announced two critical pieces of information to that group of students. First, I had shown confidence in them, believing that they could graduate. And secondly, perhaps most importantly, I had promised to stick it out with them for as long as it took to see a high school graduate in Grise Fiord. These students were accustomed to seeing teachers leave each year, only to have to get to know another group of new teachers the following year. The idea of having the same teacher for all of their high school years was unfathomable, yet here someone was promising just that. I had not planned to state this intention that day – the words jumped out of my mouth before I could think. My subconscious knew we would stay in Grise Fiord until Umimmak School produced its first high school graduate.

As more and more specific questions arose, I told them there would be lots of time to learn all of the details they wanted to know. We had talked for over an hour, long enough for our first meeting. I left it up to the students to decide how they wanted their work area arranged and who would sit beside whom. I moved aside and let them talk amongst themselves as they noisily moved furniture around the room. It only took a few minutes to get everything the way they wanted. As soon as the desks were in place, they all sat down at their new seats and waited. They seemed eager to begin. I could see we had gotten off to a good start.

Considering the cross-cultural setting of non-Inuit teachers in an Inuit community, I had learned it is very important to introduce students and community members to new teachers in a non-threatening, comfortable environment. For many Inuit, this means outside, not in the stuffy confines of a southern-styled school. To start school off with kids sitting at desks for a full day of indoor lessons would be extremely difficult for both the students and the new teachers. It is hard for students to suddenly become indoor creatures after a long summer of freedom and outdoor activity living on the land. Therefore, on our first school day, after meeting in the classroom for the morning, we spent the entire afternoon at a community picnic.

We hiked from the school up the gravel road toward the airstrip with all of the students, carrying boxes of hotdogs, juice, tea, and biscuits, as well as Coleman stoves, fuel, kettles, foam cups, and plastic forks needed for everyone in town. Parents had joined us at the school to help students carry all the supplies. Harry and Geela, the school office manager, had made bilingual announcements on the radio to let everyone know where and when the picnic would be held. Most of the local places of work were allowing their employees to take time off during the afternoon to attend the festivity. Members of the District Education Authority (DEA), locally elected school officials, were on hand to welcome the teachers to the community and to start off the celebration.

Very quickly, scrap wood that had been collected in town from crates and discarded piles of construction materials was thrown into a heap and soon a roaring campfire was ready for roasting hotdogs on sticks. Coleman stoves were set up and water from the river boiled for tea. Everyone milled around the fire and began chatting with each other in Inuktitut. YoAnne and I strolled between groups of parents and children to smile and say hello. We spoke what little Inuktitut we could but switched into English fairly quickly. *We would get better!* we told everyone. As soon as every-one had their fill of hotdogs, and juice or tea, the soccer balls and Frisbees were brought out and children scattered over the rocky plateau to burn off energy. Some adults joined in on the games; most stayed near the fire to chat with friends. It was a glorious af-ternoon. The sun was shining and the gentlest breeze swept over the land. Even though this particular memory is years past, I re-member staring at the deep blue sky above the mountains near the river valley. I don't think I've ever seen blue sky like that anywhere else.

Four years isn't a long time to an adult, but to a child, four years is an eternity. Children and young adults grow and change incredibly during that amount of time. I've thought back to that first morning in my classroom at Umimmak School and the af-ternoon picnic – many times – remembering so many faces and voices, and I marvel at how their lives developed over the years and at how quickly some of those children became young adults. Over the years some teaching staff left, some left and returned, new ones joined us. In my second year I became principal of Umimmak School and inevitably the grade 10 class evolved to be-come a grade 10-11 class. In my last year at the school, that original grade 10 classroom had become the grade 10-11-12 classroom – an eclectic group of wonderful senior high students. I am proud to have been part of their education.

4

The Cycle of the School Seasons

Inuit culture is inextricably linked to the natural environment. Inuit are connected in very real ways to the land and to the seasonal changes that occur throughout the year. As much as is possible, school programming needs to accommodate and reflect this reliance on and connection to the natural world. The natural cycle of the seasons should be reflected to a large extent in the program of any Inuit school. Each season brings with it a character and very specific school activities.

After teaching in two Arctic communities before arriving in Grise Fiord, I was convinced that whatever the important parts of the prescribed academic curriculum were, as much as possible had to be completed between September and December. This was especially true at the senior high level. Older students are more likely able to focus on the day-to-day rhythm of school during this time. Attendance is almost always best during the first term. Students are keen and ready for school after the long summer. As much as we educators seem to think that January to April is a good time for covering a lot of academics, time flies by far too quickly after the Christmas break. Before you know it, spring arrives and more land-based teaching and outdoor activities begin. Although many shorter school-based land trips occur in the fall, before the colder weather sets in, there is much more of a focus on regular academic class work.

It is crucial, however, that time be given at the beginning of the school year for all-important rapport and team-building activities. Activities planned for the first few days of school are also designed to involve as many community members as possible. As an example, community picnics, like the one I described in Grise Fiord, occur in most Nunavut communities within the first few days of school.

During the next three years of our stay in Grise, we organized a scavenger hunt for the first week back at school. It became a popular school tradition. Teams of multi-aged students, kindergarten to grade 12, tried to gather as many items on a list as possible. The purpose of the "hunt" was to have students work together to accomplish a goal and to orient themselves about the school within the community. New school staff, too, learned about their new community.

Even though the students had lived in Grise their entire lives, many did not know a lot about how their community functioned. Students were sent to the far reaches of the hamlet to collect items such as different sized and coloured rocks, construction materials such as screws and nails, animal bones, and so on. License plate numbers were recorded for specific town vehicles. Students were also asked to collect signatures from all current DEA members – this meant they needed to find out who was on the council and then search them out. This task enabled students to create a formal connection with the DEA from the very start of the school year. Students were also asked to gather signatures of the Hamlet councillors. Various tidbits of information about teachers (birth dates, favourite foods, and eye colour) were included on the list. Other items to be searched out included Band-Aids (from the Health Centre); weather information (from the Airport Authority); various municipal facts, such as the number of litres in the town's water storage silo; and the polar bear quota for the year (from the

Hunters and Trappers Organization). This encouraged students to learn about their community from different perspectives and to interact with a wide array of people. But the main thing was the scavenger hunt was a fun, non-threatening school event where students could actively participate with their friends.

Many teachers coming from the south believe they must start teaching the curriculum as quickly as possible, particularly with senior secondary students. Educators are continually drilled in the importance of covering all of the curricular outcomes necessary for each grade level. I discovered early on, however, that in a second-language, cross-cultural setting it is much more important to get to know one another first and to have a bit of fun. I observed that teachers who spent time at the beginning of the year involving themselves and their students in enjoyable, educational activities designed to teach themselves about one another were much more likely to be successful in encouraging these same students to take risks in their learning early on in the classroom. I found that participating in hands-on classroom activities requiring little use of English helped to establish the new teacher as someone who appreciates the difficulties of learning in a second language.

Most seasoned northern teachers agree that a sincere interest in learning about Inuit culture and Inuktitut language goes a long way in developing credibility and respect with their students and the community. It is critical for a teacher to show a willingness to learn from their students. If the curriculum is not followed exactly during those first couple of weeks of school, it is not the end of the world – there are more immediate and important tasks at hand. This is a difficult lesson for a lot of educators to learn. We are conditioned through teacher education programs to use curriculum documents as our reference point for everything we do in the classroom. I too have been described as a teacher with a strong program orientation but the extent to which I rely on the details of the curriculum truly varies greatly from class to class, year to year. The reality is that some curricular outcomes are covered more in one year than another.

At the beginning of the school year, a few days were always

missed early on, with the arrival of the sealift ship. The oil and gas tankers would arrive close to the same time, to replenish the fuel silos for the year. Every truck, snowmobile, and ATV needed gasoline; each business, agency, and home needed oil for heat over the coming year.

Sealift arrival is a huge community event, lasting two to four days, and school has to close while goods are offloaded from barges onto flatbed trucks on the shore. Almost all of the yearly supplies for the school arrived via sealift as well. Several crates needed to be delivered and unpacked on the school steps. A collective sigh of relief can be felt throughout the community after the ships depart. There is great satisfaction knowing that the community is well stocked for the coming months.

As with many other schools in Canada, Arctic schools celebrate all major Christian traditions associated with the calendar year – Thanksgiving, Christmas, and Easter. Almost all students in the small communities scattered across Nunavut are Inuit whose families worship in Christian churches. Although students learn about multiculturalism and the wide range of world religions, many of the actual school celebrations conform to the Christian tradition. The routines of the school year centre on nature's seasons as well as the advancing and passing of these holidays.

After the first few settling-in weeks, students' thoughts turn to Thanksgiving. It seems odd yet brightly coloured cut-out drawings of turkeys and pumpkins adorn even Arctic classroom and hallway walls. Parents organize huge family meals, enjoying turkey and pumpkin pie as much as caribou, muskox, seal, and "Inuit ice cream," a mixture of berries and sweetened caribou suet. A community feast in the gymnasium followed by games and other activities cap off the holiday weekend.

During our first year in Grise Fiord, YoAnne and I dined on roast polar bear for our Thanksgiving meal. Mimi, the elementary teacher, was the first of the season to successfully hunt a bear. That very night, the animal was skinned and butchered right there on the cold, dark beach lit by strategically placed lanterns and the headlights of parked snowmobiles. We were struck with how human-like the bear appeared after being skinned. The steam rose from the exposed flesh, forming a veiled mist over the immediate area. Anyone who wanted to was encouraged to help with the cutting, dividing and bagging up of the meat. Generous portions were allotted to the Elders first, then the rest was shared with anyone who wanted to take some meat home. The good fortune of the timely hunt was celebrated by everyone in town.

Many at the shore that evening shared their favourite recipes with us. Polar bear meat is the one flesh that needs to be cooked well. It is never eaten raw like seal, caribou, or muskox. Polar bears are at the top of the food chain so any contaminants are greatly magnified within their body systems. YoAnne and I lugged two heavy plastic Co-op bags stuffed with bloody bear meat up the stairs to our apartment. We were so excited by this rare opportunity we videotaped the unpacking of the bags of meat right away. Having lived in the North a few years by then, we had never tried polar bear. Not really knowing what to expect, our meal the next day was surprisingly good – polar bear tastes like lamb. Delicious.

Not long after Thanksgiving, the cut-outs on the walls transform into bats, witches, and ghosts in preparation for All Hallows' Eve. I have never seen Hallowe'en celebrated to the extent it is in the North. Toddlers, youths, adolescents, adults, and Elders all got into the ghoulish spirit. Elders I had never seen outside of their homes went trick-or-treating. Similar to mummering in Newfoundland, one of the goals in this tradition of visiting houses is to disguise yourself in such a way that your host does not recognize you. Children and Elders alike derive huge amounts of pleasure if you cannot guess who they are through their costumes as they stand at your door with candy sacks opened wide.

Another thing I always found curious is that often the first big blizzard of the season happened on October 31. This never stopped the ghouls' visits though. Later in the evening, games are played and competitions held for the entire community in the gymnasium. For Hallowe'en in Grise Fiord, many of the girls and women dressed as men, while the boys and men dressed as women. Participants were very creative with their outfits and acted completely uninhibited, the boys in particular. Peals of laughter rang out over the evening competitions for "best dressed as the opposite sex." One year, a grade 9 student won first place. Manasie was one of the most quiet, shy boys in the school, yet he donned a blonde wig, halter-top, tight skirt, and stockings for the community to gaze upon. He was tall, slim, and gorgeous. My impression of Manasie at that moment completely changed. I wasn't aware of his wonderful sense of humour, nor of his courage as a young adolescent to act silly knowing that he would be the focus of great laughter. Manasie showed a confidence in himself I had not seen in school. I was reminded that I might never truly know these students, unless I spent time with them outside of school, as they went about their real, authentic lives.

Hallowe'en is significant in Grise Fiord for another reason. It marks the last days of the sun for nearly three and a half months. Sometime near October 31, the sun dips below the horizon and does not reappear until the second week of February. A perpetual sunset dominates the sky for weeks in mid-October through mid-November, and at the other end of the dark season, a persistent sunrise. For the two months in between, day-to-day life carries on in complete darkness. You literally cannot see the keyhole in your door when you go home for lunch each day.

Many people have asked me how I coped with the darkness. I always tell them it is not nearly as terrible as most people imagine. It is a restful, tranquil time of the year. Think of that feeling you get in the evening hours in the south, just before bedtime – that sense of calm serenity. That is the only way I can describe the dark period. I never disliked it at all. Although we still worked, people tended to hunker down and cocoon at this time. I was thankful, however, when the light began to return, as were the Inuit inhabitants of these northern communities.

Christmas is the single most celebrated holiday in contemporary Inuit life. Schools begin decorating for the holiday season the day after Hallowe'en, and this constant state of decorating does not stop until the actual school holiday. The interior of the school is transformed into something that resembles Santa's workshop

– every available vertical space is plastered with colourful images of the Big Elf himself, Christmas trees and wrapped gifts, teddy bears, toboggans, snowmen, and snowmobiles. Streamers cross the ceilings of each classroom; tinsel and strings of popcorn cling to anything standing; it was rare to *not* hear carols being played from some corner of the school. As we enter the dark period, it seems that every house throughout the community suddenly becomes lit up with vibrant displays of red, green, white, and blue. These colourful decorations throughout the hamlet warm both homes and hearts.

Many Inuit are devout Christians and take the birth of Christ as a solemn yet joyous occasion to celebrate. In fact, Christmas becomes the focus of the school program for a large portion of November and December, more so in the early grades. In Grise Fiord, young children are especially excited at this time of year, knowing that since they live in the community closest to the North Pole, they are the first to be visited by the jolly, red-dressed man on Christmas Eve. Even Elders take turns to sit on his knee as he occupies his place in the big chair in the corner of the gymnasium early in the evening.

The activities of this particular holiday season cement together the school and community like no other – the only possible exception being the onset of spring camping. At Christmas, both the school and community work together on many projects – the Christmas Eve feast in the community hall (the school gym in smaller hamlets), the stage preparations and presentation of the annual school concert, the organization of the nightly music, dancing, and games played in the gym throughout the break. The school itself is host to many of the indoor community events of the holiday season.

A curious thing happens in Arctic communities at Christmas. During the two-week school break, everyone in the community assumes a reversed daytime-nighttime schedule. Beginning on Christmas Day, each resident of the hamlet makes their way down to the gym for seven o'clock in the evening to play games, often until eight or nine the following morning. Most games involve throwing dice into a large circle of people. Upon throwing the lucky number, the player races to the centre to either unwrap lay-ered-and-taped packages while wearing oven mitts, or to dress themselves with as many clothes as possible in an impossible pile, or put together a giant jigsaw puzzle ... or similar types of fun. Other games required much running back and forth, in relay, from one end of the gym to the other to deposit a dangling nail attached to the back of your pants into an empty pop can, to spin around a broom handle multiple times, to knock over a stand of cans with a bean bag, to push a ball with your nose ... you get the picture! Musical chairs involving the entire room was a favourite as well.

Games were periodically punctuated with accordion and gui-tar music and square dancing. Adults would dance in circles into the wee hours of the morning, and the youngest children would be mimicking them in smaller circles all around the gym. Eventual-ly, each family headed home for a sleep. But they soon rise again in time for a quick bite to eat, before heading out for yet another day's festivities. Many events are held on the ice along the shore during the dark days of the holiday season. Harpoon throwing and seal hunting contests are very popular, as are the competitions for ice carvings and outdoor Christmas light displays throughout the hamlet.

What never ceased to amaze me was how every single mem-ber of the community participated in all of these activities. From toddlers barely able to stand, to school-aged children, to mothers and fathers, to other adults and Elders – no one missed out on the joy and excitement (as well as the resultant deafening noise level in the gym) of celebrating good times together over the Christmas holiday.

This busy time-warping routine continues daily until after the New Year's snowmobile parade through town. After ringing in the New Year at the gym, everyone would hop on their snow-mobiles and follow a leader, single file, throughout the town – up and down each road, around homes and buildings and then out onto the sea ice. What a sight it must have been to see from above: a long winding snake of lights slithering in the dark over the Arctic tundra and sea. After the short fireworks display, the snowmobiles would carry everyone to their homes in time for the New Year's radio call-in show. Despite seeing everyone each day over the previous two weeks, New Year's wishes were broadcast to individuals and families throughout the hamlet. Of course, people called other community radio stations as well, to give good wishes to family and friends afar.

Needless to say, by the time work and school begin again in January, every resident is exhausted and it takes nearly another two weeks for everyone to get their daytime-nighttime schedules back on track. This has huge implications for the school program. The lessons taught in early January need to be self-contained so that students can catch up easily and are not too far behind. One Christmas season in particular had YoAnne and I playing games most nights with everyone else in town. Our schedules too became "upside-down." That first week back in school in January was difficult, to say the least. We were flat-out tired, every single day. But we honestly and completely understood what the students were going through.

Every person, Inuit or non-Inuit, celebrates the rising of the sun. The New Year in Grise Fiord is marked by a change in the quality of light in the southern sky. Although still dark throughout the day, a hint of the light soon to come over the next five weeks or so teases the hearts of Arctic dwellers.

I was asked one February, live on CBC television's *Midday* show, to articulate the feeling of seeing the sun rise for the first time in months and to describe the colours in the sky as it was happening. There were no TV cameras to record the event. Viewers heard only my voice speaking over a map of the eastern Arctic. Prior to the main event, the sky directly over Devon Island was a pastel hue of pink and orange. Magnificent. Thin fog hovered over the island's ice cap, producing a fuzzy, out-of-focus appearance to the lower sky. Just as I was thinking the ice crystals would obscure the sun's brief appearance that day, a sliver of brilliant yellow peeked out of the fog with a blinding intensity. It lasted only a few minutes and then began to sink below the horizon once again.

How did it make me feel? Tina, the host, asked. Uplifted, light in spirit, optimistic, free, and exhilarated! And everyone in town felt the same way. This was the beginning of the journey into the light period. Hunting, camping – a full life on the land would resume again.

Students had been decorating the walls of the school this time with bright suns and colourful rainbows. They had also been trying to guess the exact minute in the hour of the day that the sun would show itself. Each year a contest was held to see who could guess the correct time of the first sunrise in February. Students wrote down their guesses before CBC Radio announced the expected time of the sun's arrival. Technology unfortunately has taken the mystique out of some of nature's mysteries. Several local hunters were able to determine this coveted information from their GPSs ahead of time.

Valentine's Day sees red hearts plastered all over the school. Even though the sun has returned for almost a week, it is still frigid outside, and most activity remains indoors. Easter sees pastel-coloured eggs and cute rabbits adorning every nook and cranny of the building. Easter is also the time of year when the Hamlet organizes games and a huge feast down on the ice in front of the community. By then, the weather has warmed up enough so that if you were properly dressed you could spend several hours outside, even the younger children. Dog sled races, snowmobiles pulling huge empty oil drums on *qamouti* (sleds), tug-o-war contests, ptarmigan and seal hunting competitions, and harpoon throwing are all offered, with much coveted prizes of sleeping bags, stoves, jerry cans, gasoline, and the like.

The Easter festival is the first big community event after Christmas and marks the true start of the spring season where most men, often with their families, begin to spend a lot more time "out on the land," camping and hunting. Outfitters would already be busy taking sport hunters from all over the world on trips during the previous month. By April, young families too can enjoy extended camping trips to their favourite places. In my experience, most Easter weekends brought agreeable weather. Short of a full-blown blizzard, however, these games would not be hastily cancelled.

By mid-April, twenty-four-hour daylight comes to the hamlet. In order to sleep, most people tape aluminum foil on their bedroom windows to keep out the light. Even a pin-prick in the foil can blind you if you wake in the middle of the night facing the window. It is amazing the amount of energy that people get when it is constantly light outside. During my first few years in the North, I would catch myself vacuuming the house or baking cookies well into the early hours of the morning. I simply did not want to go to bed. Children wander in the streets, playing with friends and visiting each other's houses throughout the entire night.

I lost track of the number of evenings I forced myself to bed, listening to the sounds of children not far from my window. For me the light period was more difficult to adjust to than the dark period. It seems the sun returns faster than your body can properly adapt. Thank goodness for polarized sunglasses! The sun, combined with the reflective properties of the snow and ice, produces a blinding light, even when clouds move in. Sometimes the flat light produced through ice crystals or low-lying cloud is harder on your eyes than the direct light of a clear day. The period between mid-April and the end of the school year, for all intents and purposes, is one very long day – a day when everyone is in good spirit and spends their life in the out of doors.

As much as possible, land-based activities are offered by the school at this time of year. It just makes sense. Different classes or groups of students spend entire days or half days out on the land. Snowmobiles and *qamouti* are rounded up, with stoves, tents, and the various supplies needed in case of sudden bad weather. Outfitters, licensed guides, and volunteer parents are all involved in the land-based program of the school. While the school owns a small amount of outdoor equipment, most of the snowmobiles, *qamouti* and many of the other supplies needed for these trips are loaned to the school by community members. Even the "ambulance" *qamoutik*, the sled with a white box and red cross, was loaned to the school by the Health Centre on many occasions.

Parents always join students and staff in these activities. Older students generally go out first, until it's warm enough for the primary and elementary students to be able to withstand the cold for prolonged times. These trips may be as simple as walking out onto the sea ice towards a nearby iceberg for tea and freshly cooked bannock. Sometimes snowmobiles and *qamouti* take students up the fiord to look for animal tracks, or to sight some Arctic hare and ptarmigan. Traditional land skills are taught in the Inuktitut language to students by the guides, all of whom are skilled hunters. Students participate in building snow shelters and igloos; they learn how to navigate according to wind and snow drift patterns; they are shown how to hunt for seals and ptarmigan. Students learn how to pack a *qamoutik* and how to cook bannock.

Each year in Grise Fiord, a small group of students participated in a hunt for *umimmak*, muskox. The Hunters and Trappers Organization (HTO) awarded two tags to the school for this much anticipated annual event. Experienced hunters led the small group of students (boys and girls, usually from the junior and senior high classes) along with three or four teachers on the day's excursion. Extra fuel, food, tents, and sleeping gear was always packed in the event of unforeseen circumstances. In the Arctic, even in May, you never know! A long lead, or large crack, in the ice can halt a convoy of snowmobiles until the new water freezes; a storm can blow in at any time; the hunt may take longer than expected. In Grise Fiord, muskoxen are usually found on the grassy flat areas at the base of the mountains by the sea, a few hours drive to the east. Amazingly, it is the lichens and mosses beneath the snow that nourishes these large animals throughout the winter.

Students are taught how to track the muskox, where to aim and then shoot one, as well as skinning, butchering and packing up the large pieces of meat to transport back to the community. Many students have seen this before, accompanying family members on such trips, but for some, this is their first muskox hunt. What a learning experience it was for me and YoAnne and any other *qallunaaq* lucky enough to be able to join in on the field trip. I must admit the first time I saw a muskox, I was surprised at how short they are – a huge wooly animal, with a massive horned head, but only about five feet at the shoulders. However, seeing a herd of them in the circular defensive position, tails in, heads out, was quite impressive.

As the guide quizzed the students on the body parts and internal organ systems, steam rose from the carcass, enabling mitten-less hands to poke, cut, skin, and bag up the various cuts. The full head and fur skin too were rolled and tied onto the *qamoutik*. All the while, boys and girls excitedly asked questions, giggled, and helped with whatever needed doing. By the time we returned to town, very late in the evening, parents, children, and Elders met us on the shore in front of the school to greet the successful hunters. As usual, the Elders received bags of meat to take home and the rest was divided up amongst the other families. The fur was eventually stretched and dried and then used in later land activities for the school.

The largest component of the land program is the annual spring camp. Weeks in advance a committee of parents, teachers, and DEA members is formed to plan for the week-long camping trip for all junior and senior high students. Any community member can join in on the camp; in fact, most of the younger students end up participating as well since their entire family goes out with the school. Shorter trips from the school are organized daily for those kindergarten to grade 6 students whose parents do not go to the overnight camp.

Each year the DEA consults with the community through call-in radio programs to decide where the camp will take place. The location is particularly important because it has to offer good fishing and hunting and be a safe site for children. The community also likes the children to visit culturally significant areas. One year the camp was set up twenty-five kilometres from town, midway between Grise Fiord and the large cape to the south. A site on Devon Island was chosen the following year – a trip that took sixteen hours by snowmobile. One year, an inland site bordering a lake for ice fishing was chosen. Students were always very excited at this time of year. While most of them did camp regularly with their families, a few did not so this was an opportunity for those students in particular to spend time on the land learning traditional skills.

Once out on the land, non-Inuit teachers usually take a back seat in these spring camp activities. It is a prime opportunity for *qallunaat* to allow their students to teach them something. More often than not, it is the non-academic students in the classroom – the ones who do not experience success often – who shine and excel out on the land. While struggling in science, Terry could handle his own dog team; Manasie had great difficulty with mathematics but I trusted him with my life on the land. He was mature, dependable, and always knew what needed doing in any situation. Spring camp provides teachers with the opportunity to discover other facets of their students' characters, away from the confines of the school environment. Spring camp is also a time of humility as students observe their teachers trying new things that may not come very easily. The tables are turned. I was always impressed with the patience and maturity that even younger students exhibited while teaching others new skills.

Once, while on a long-distance day trip, we had stopped for tea and our guide had decided to hunt for a seal so we could have fresh meat for our supper. As our hunter bent over a seal-breathing hole for what seemed like hours, eight-year-old Pauline decided to teach me some Inuit string games. *Ayarak* is similar to what southerners know as "cat's cradle," yet much more intricate. Pauline wanted me to learn how to make a caribou walk over the tundra – a "moving" string pattern. I tried my best but I struggled. It was hopeless. I never did get the hang of it. Pauline laughed and laughed – she could toss her hands up in the air, move her fingers almost imperceptibly and all of a sudden, a caribou would be travelling from her right hand towards her left, across an imaginary tundra. It was me who eventually gave up, not Pauline.

In Pangnirtung and Hall Beach, school-organized spring camp activities occurred in April. Being much further north, spring camp usually takes place during the third week of May in Grise Fiord. Any later the snow and ice conditions could prove dangerous for travelling groups with young children. The time that remains in the school year is very difficult to plan – students would much prefer to stay outside. For the younger classes, teachers still take students out of the school regularly for walks and fresh air. Physical education classes at this time of year are either cross-country skiing or baseball, or any other such outdoor pursuit. It was always a trying time for the senior students in the school. They needed to keep focused for a bit longer as they continued to earn credits towards their diploma.

At Umimmak School, we managed to schedule final examinations prior to spring camp. This was always a challenge, but it was unrealistic to believe that academics could carry on after the camp. Therefore, short, intensive, one-credit courses were offered to the junior and senior high students for the remaining three weeks or so in the school year. They could choose from options such as silk-screen printing, jewelry-making, computer troubleshooting, traditional sewing, qamoutik building, and a myriad of other high-interest, hands-on activities.

No school year is complete without the end-of-school assembly, where students are rewarded for their efforts and proud parents sit in the gymnasium audience with, at that time, videotape rolling. In Grise Fiord, the entire community attended. In the school itself, once the tables and chairs were moved into the hallway for the summer cleaning and all of the classroom bulletin boards cleared, students could barely contain themselves as they eagerly looked toward to those long school-free days of summer. Before we knew it, the last day of school was upon us and we were all contemplating how quickly the year had passed. Thoughts begin to wander toward the next school year. *What will we do again? What will we do differently? How can we do better?* And so goes the cycle of the seasons at Umimmak School, Grise Fiord, Nunavut.

5

The First Ever High School Class

Looking back over my four years in Grise Fiord, I smile as I picture myself in the high school classroom, facing all of those excited young people in the early days of grade 10. I learned so much from them. Even now, two decades after leaving Nunavut, I am keenly aware that the time spent teaching there was life-changing. The years in Grise Fiord were especially wonderful. I began high school again, alongside my students. I experienced the challenges and joys of difficult work and pride in achievement. I shared much emotion with these young people during those first few years of the new high school program.

Most non-teachers are unaware of how even the most experienced educator feels at the start of a new school year. I know teachers with twenty-five or more years in the profession who endure sleepless nights, constant worrying, and stomach upset for a full week prior to that first day back. Every class is so different. One of the hardest parts of teaching is getting to know new students at the beginning of September (August in Nunavut), especially if you are new to the community. *Where do I begin? How can*

I quickly develop a respectful rapport? Those first few interactions are so important. No pressure.

The first activity we tackled together in the classroom was a personal writing exercise. Being the homeroom teacher of a grade 10 group of young adults, ranging in age from sixteen to twenty, as well as teaching them most other subjects during the day, I needed to learn about them as individuals as fast as possible. I also needed to determine where each of them was with respect to their English language skills. An advantage of teaching the same group of students all day is that you can be as flexible as needed within the daily schedule. Early in the year, most senior high school schedules change often anyway, as timetables are adapted and improved upon. I allowed several full mornings for them to complete the writing exercise, as the time spent on this particular activity early in the term would pay off later on.

I asked them to write their life stories. Dead silence. Before panic set in, I immediately went about *showing* them my own life story. I brought out a long roll of paper instead of loose-leaf sheets. They drew nearer, curious to see what I had done. I had prepared a timeline, representing my life, on the long sheet of brown butcher's paper. I unrolled it and began telling my story starting in the year of my birth and working up through the years to my arrival in Grise Fiord. I had marked in what I considered important events in my life – visiting the swans by the river in England, hill-walking as a preschooler in Scotland, framing my first drawing, immigrating to Canada as a child with my family, moving to the lake, entering university, walking transects for a bird survey, on safari in Africa, becoming a park naturalist, teaching in Pangnirtung, and so on. Needless to say, they were interested in learning about the details of my life. I answered many questions. I consciously monitored how I was modelling the activity – after all, I expected them to do the very same thing over the next few days.

I explained the information gathered by each student would later be written up as a story on the computer, printed out, and put into book form. Each of their stories would be a chapter in the book entitled *Our Lives*. They smiled and seemed to like the idea, excited at the prospect of authoring their own stories. They understood that the timeline idea would help them to organize the details of their lives. The computers were new to the school, a result of extra funding for the program extension into senior secondary schooling, and had not yet been unpacked and set up. They were anxious to be the first to use them.

They paired up quickly, cut long pieces of paper from the roll, claimed a space on the floor or at a nearby table, and immediately drew a long straight line with a ruler down the centre of each of their sheets. There was lots of chatter, mostly in Inuktitut, as students began talking about their early childhood. Sometimes, a voice would be heard over all the others exclaiming, "No! That was *after* you moved from Pond Inlet." Or "Yes, that was the year I broke my arm." Or "Remember when ..." They constantly asked each other for help in recollecting their own specific life events. Almost all of them had grown up with each other from birth and were able to verify the times and confirm the details as they proceeded. This process took two or three mornings to complete. Each student had started their timeline with the year of their birth and then, with brightly coloured markers, added in events such as "baby brother born," "got sick with chickenpox," "moved into new house," "grandfather died," "made my first caribou *kamiks*," and so on. Afterwards, they walked amongst all of the timelines displayed on the floor, encouraging each other and remembering some of the shared memories identified by their friends.

The next step was to write out the first draft of their life events on paper, adding or taking away as they thought best. In order to help them write more than just a chronological listing of their life events, I encouraged them to include the emotions they experienced throughout those events. *How did I feel when that happened?* They went through the process of writing that first draft, proofreading each other's work, and editing before writing the second and third drafts on the computers. Before the end of September, after a lot of hard work, three copies of *Our Lives* were printed, put in green duo tangs and placed on the bookmobile in the classroom. I encouraged them to simply pick up one of the books whenever they had a free moment and read at their leisure. Students were very proud of themselves and did not object to having the stories on display for parent-teacher meetings and open houses early in the fall. Throughout the year, younger students from other classes were "given permission" by my students to read the stories as well. Even well into their third year in high school, those same green duo tangs were pulled off the shelf and browsed through, often eliciting broad smiles from the readers.

Through this particular exercise, not only did I determine the levels of English skills of my new students, but I also quickly learned much about their individual lives as well as some important community events. Russell had been bitten by a fox as a young child and went through the horror of receiving rabies shots. Manasie was adopted as a toddler in Iqaluit. Both Gayle and Jeffrey had moved to Grise from Arctic Bay and Pond Inlet. Susie was pregnant with Jeffrey's baby. Some of my students' relatives had recently moved to Inukjuaq in northern Quebec. I was pleasantly surprised by the variety of information discussed within the class throughout this activity.

Writing is difficult for most students, especially those learning in a second language situation. Students learned that writing is a process, not simply an end product. More notably they learned that autobiographical writing allowed them to comfortably disclose information about themselves and that taking risks in school could be a lot of fun. They learned that their lives were important and of interest to others. After seeing the success of this activity, I often asked students to document specific times in their lives and to write about them. They always seemed willing to share their real-life stories. With practise they eventually began to write more creative, fictional tales as well.

Because I had these students most of the day, I could integrate many subject areas into themes and project-based activities. I was a teacher of language more than anything else though. Every single lesson, regardless of the subject area, was preceded by an ESL (English as a Second Language) strategy. Students needed help navigating the specialized vocabulary of subjects like science and mathematics in particular, and also with complex wording in social studies and with the English language in general. I remember asking a student to define what I thought to be a simple word, yet I was met with a blank stare. I learned that the word I was looking for was not the problem. The student did not know what I meant by *define*. I had a similar encounter with the word *occur* – the student knew the answer to the question I had posed, but could not answer right away as she did not understand the word *occur*. Even though I had taught in the Baffin, I found I had to constantly remind myself that language is taught first and foremost, and only after that can attention be given to the subject content areas. Reviewing new vocabulary, playing with word puzzles, and engaging in active word games helped students feel comfortable at the beginning of new units regardless of the specific subject. Group spelling competitions, for fun, and trivia games were activities that all my senior students enjoyed a great deal.

Many critics of small community high schools claim that students are not given the same choice in course selection afforded their larger community counterparts. To a large extent this is true. A small staff is limited in their ability to offer a wide variety of courses. At Umimmak School almost all of the courses at the senior high level were general level courses. We simply did not have the staff to offer both general and academic level teaching. Individual teacher strengths change from year to year, depending on who stays and who leaves. Course schedules change annually to reflect the varying needs of the individual students in fulfilling the requirements to graduate. Schedules in small northern schools are nothing if not creative.

During my four years at Umimmak School, we managed to offer nearly fifty different courses to the senior students. In their first year of high school, they were given the opportunity to earn over thirty-five credits, the recommended number of credits needed to enter grade 11. Along with English, general science, mathematics, and social studies, students were taught northern studies, career and life management, art, and physical education. The assignments of the teaching staff in all small northern communities are somewhat eclectic. Often a hole in the schedule needs to be filled, and any member of the staff may be asked to teach any number of classes outside of their specialty. I taught all of the above subjects except for social studies (Harry, the principal for that first year, came in for those classes). Harry was also teaching some of the junior high courses to YoAnne's class. I taught ESL and math to the grade 3-4-5 class three or four times a week so that Mimi could teach my students Inuktitut. Mostly though, I spent the vast majority of my time in that first year with the grade 10 class.

For three weeks before Christmas and another three weeks the following May, students were offered even more choices of courses. The "academics" were put on hold and one-credit, CTS modules (career and technological studies) were made available to the junior and senior high classes. The junior high students were included so numbers involved in the various courses were reasonable. They were allowed to "bank" credits until they themselves reached grade 10. It also gave both groups an opportunity to interact with each other in high-interest courses. Maintaining student interest during the few weeks before Christmas and at the end of the school year was difficult, so these short twenty-five-hour modules gave students a welcome change in their schedules as well as a chance to earn credits quickly. Using the strengths of the available staff, students chose amongst diverse modules such as mining, 2-D design, keyboarding, word processing, leadership, and income tax (yes ... income tax!). Students also earned a credit for participating in the annual spring camp.

Each year, more core courses at higher skill levels were offered to students, as well as elective credits and additional CTS modules. These modules were offered each year in ever increasing increments of difficulty. For example, students were given more and more responsibility and tasks at each spring camp; therefore, they earned beginning, intermediate and advanced CTS credits for their work. Likewise, by their third year at the secondary level, some students could troubleshoot many computer problems and earned advanced credits in technology. Students also needed to earn a community service credit in order to graduate high school. This involved a minimum of twenty-five hours of work within the community. This was probably the easiest credit earned as the community was always happy to have students work on projects at the various agencies in town.

In my second year in Grise Fiord, Harry and his wife left the North and I became the principal of Umimmak School. YoAnne and I left the Health Centre apartment and moved in to the "principal's house" at the far end of town. I continued to teach math, science, and art. I also taught health and personal development along with a number of CTS modules throughout the year. Stephen, previously teaching Inuit in northern Quebec, was hired to teach the senior students English, social studies, and physical education as well as a number of junior high and elementary classes. YoAnne continued mainly with math and science at the junior high level, but she also taught French to the senior class. The community of Grise Fiord has a historical link to Inuit of northern Quebec and students showed great interest in learning French. YoAnne's first language is French (she hails from St. Jérôme, Quebec). Since she had earned a double major in science and French, she was more than happy to introduce her language to the students.

Each year new teachers were hired with differing specialties and interests and the elective courses offered reflected this diversity in staff backgrounds. When the school was awarded an extra half-time teaching position, the school schedules became even more malleable. I was then able to spend more needed time on my administrative duties. Stephen left the community after one year and was replaced by Vincent, who had previously taught in the western Arctic. Mimi went on leave and was replaced by Krista. Krista's partner, Cory, also took a half-time position teaching the junior high class. By this time, YoAnne had cut back to a half-time position with the school and had kept her half-time Nunavut Arctic College adult education job as well. She piloted a very popular peer-helping course, *Aulajaatut*, to the high school students that year.

Vincent, Krista, and Cory all left at the end of that year and in year four we were joined by Andrea and Tammy. Tammy came to us from a First Nations school in Manitoba. She took the junior high class, but since she was a certified physical education teacher (our first at Umimmak School), she also taught the gym classes for the senior students. Andrea had spent the previous year working at a girls' home in Nepal. She was to teach the senior humanities courses, but she also showed great interest in teaching art. Although it was difficult for me to "let go" of the art, I knew Andrea would inject fresh, new ideas into the program. I never regretted passing the torch to her as she did a superb job. I also believe the students responded positively to this change. While there are many advantages to teaching the same students the same subjects each year, a drawback is that students and teachers may become too accustomed to each other's ways – sometimes a change in the routines helps to maintain interest and enthusiasm.

I mention all of these staff changes to illustrate a point. Each year, new teachers arrived. Each year, there was a period of time in the fall where students and new teachers needed to become acquainted. As a staff, we could not determine what elective courses or CTS modules would be offered each year until we got to know the personalities and expertise of any new staff members. Every year, new high school teachers had to learn about the then Northwest Territories (NWT) senior secondary program and credit system. Each year was different. The only constants for the senior students from year to year were the local instructors, as well as Yo-Anne and myself.

As a result of these annual changes, a lot of effort was put into helping the students become knowledgeable about the secondary school program and to encourage them to maintain their own records of achievement and credits earned. Of course, I maintained individual records in the office, but the students also kept their own records in their classroom, in a file they had access to and could open at any time. I designed a "graphic performance chart" for students to keep track of their course credits. One hundred squares piled up in the shape of an *inukshuk* (an Inuit stone cairn) on the page represented the hundred credits needed to graduate.

Required courses were labelled, the remainder left blank for students to label themselves. As they earned credits, the appropriate squares were coloured in. During their first year, since all of the core courses were spread out over the entire year, only the CTS modules and elective squares were filled in before the end of the year. But this was enough for them to understand that in using the chart they could visualize their path to graduation.

Any opportunity that arose where students themselves could take charge of their educational journey was explored. For example, when choices had to be made regarding course offerings, students were involved whenever possible. Senior students were always invited to school planning meetings with parents and community members. I remember consulting the high school class one spring just before the hiring for the next year was about to commence. I asked them what kind of person they wanted me to hire. The list of attributes they identified resembled many of those "effective teacher" qualities described by seasoned educators.

They wanted someone who "respected them and their culture, someone that liked the outdoors, did not shout and was not loud." They wanted someone who "knew their subject area, was interesting, and had high expectations for their students." They wanted someone "who was patient." I had half expected students to direct me to hire someone who would be easy on them. I was impressed by the seriousness with which they considered my request for help. These students never ceased to amaze me with their genuine desire to do well and to earn their right to graduate with a high school diploma. I found that the more decisions I invited the students to make, the more serious they became about their schooling. As long as they saw their decisions were being sincerely considered, they were happy offering their opinions when asked.

Despite many periodic disruptions to the school schedule, the senior class managed to maintain a general routine. I was reminded that routines are important for all students; most respond well to a moderate amount of structure. In Grise, high school classes began at 8:55 a.m. and ended at 4:20 p.m., except during our fourth year when they ended at 4:05 p.m. These hours may seem long, compared to southern schools, yet students still attended school for close to the same number of hours as would a southern student over an academic year. The extended day allowed us to close earlier in June so families could take advantage of the excellent camping weather and twenty-four-hour daylight. Individual northern communities were allowed to determine the school year calendar dates, one year at a time, as long as the required annual hours of instruction were not compromised.

Senior students shared two recesses, morning and afternoon, as well as an hour lunch each day with the K-9 students. To ensure the appropriate amount of instructional time was being spent in each of their courses, schedules were drawn up and subject areas divided into single forty-five-minute periods or doubled up into ninety-minute sessions. It was important to both students and teachers that there be a time framework in place to organize their days. These schedules were often manipulated to allow time for theme work, special interdisciplinary projects, cultural activities, or even community work.

As an example, senior students were excused each September for a day or two to help distribute the food and construction supplies that arrived on the sealift ships. Some of my male students were excused one spring for nearly a month so they could help collect fresh water in the form of chipped iceberg pieces during a serious community water shortage. Parents wanted their children to develop strong civic responsibilities and anytime the school could contribute towards this goal, students were encouraged to do so. More importantly, students were not penalized for time spent away from school. Concepts, skills, and attitudes acquired through participating in civic activity were tracked and whenever possible the students were given credit for much of their work.

While inside the school, the seniors spent most of the day within their own classroom for each subject area, except when they went to the gymnasium for physical education classes. Gym classes were usually scheduled at the same time as those of the junior high students so team sports could be played. Whenever possible, multi-age groupings within the school were encouraged, so that boys and girls of various ages could intermingle and spend time with each other. I have observed many children of various ages socializing and playing with one another in Inuit communities, more so than I have seen elsewhere. Multi-age peer groups and family groupings are commonly used in northern schools.

At Umimmak School, buddy-reading groups that always included the high school class were set up every year. The primary students would be so excited when the seniors would come into their room for the activity, they would sometimes argue a little over which high school student would be their buddy for that half-hour each week. Students took turns reading in Inuktitut and English, whichever language they wanted. At one time, a small room near the office was turned into a traditional *qammaq*, or summer shelter, by plastering the walls with old newspapers. It became a favourite place for buddy-reading. There was such a range in language skills between the older and younger students, but not always the way you would expect. One or two of the grade 4 students could read Inuktitut better than a couple of the grade 10 and 11 students. This did not appear to be a point of embarrassment for the older students though as they wisely complimented the younger ones and encouraged them to continue reading.

The senior students often went into the younger classes to help out as needed. Sometimes they would demonstrate an art activity or a science experiment. One Hallowe'en, the grade 10s practised glow-in-the-dark, mildly explosive, and smoke-producing chemistry experiments for a week before taking their show "on the road" to the other classrooms. Of course, being Hallowe'en, everyone dressed up in costumes. The sight of long-haired monsters, vagabonds, and green witches teaching a chemistry class to groups of vampires, batmen, *amauti*-clad miniature mothers (an *amautik* is a traditional parka for carrying a baby), and ballerinas is, needless to say, quite comical.

For the most part, the seniors were happy to stay in their own classroom, together as a group. They liked being the oldest students and enjoyed the perks offered to them as seniors. Many of them carried on adult lives outside of the school so it seemed reasonable to allow them certain freedoms and choices at school. The grade 10 through 12 students, for example, were the only ones allowed to smoke in the designated area outside. This was later extended to include the grade 9s as well, mostly due to the age of those specific students. The new computers were in the senior classroom, and these students were always given priority on the machines, even after school in the evenings if they chose. Likewise, because of different funding from the school board for the secondary program, the high school class received specialized art resources and various other one-time-only supplies that added to the special nature of being a high school student.

In order to maintain reasonable attendance throughout the year, the senior high schedules were always being fine-tuned and adjusted so that students were enticed to come to school regularly. Attendance is a chronic problem for most northern schools, especially at the senior level. Working for a living and receiving a paycheque is very attractive to young adults everywhere. Mandatory attendance in school only really came about in the Northwest Territories after the Education Act was changed in 1996. But even after that, there was no real way to enforce daily school attendance.

Many Inuit families still live a fairly traditional life, spending a lot of time on the land or being involved in traditional activities. Children travel with their parents for long periods of time and often help with more household duties than children of the same age in the south. Very young girls, for example, are expected to babysit even younger siblings as parents take care of other home responsibilities. Many young boys are encouraged to learn hunting skills early on in their lives and miss school whenever an opportunity arises to go on the land. Older students often have children of their own, or part-time jobs in the community, or an array of other reasons to miss school. Educators must constantly remind students and their parents why school is important, especially a high school education. The students need to feel that their learning is meaningful, with purpose and of use to them in their lives. Curriculum may need to be molded a little – or changed a lot – to meet the needs of the students within the individual communities.

While I taught in Grise Fiord, attendance at Umimmak School was better than most of the other schools in the Baffin. In my monthly reports to the Board, very rarely did the overall attendance dip below the 80 percent level. The primary and elementary classes almost always reported over 90 percent attendance. For years, long before I arrived, the community had supported the school fairly positively and sent their children there on a regular basis. I worried, however, that like most high schools in the North, the attendance would begin to slip after the novelty wore off. Of course, there are always certain times in the year when attendance is extremely difficult to maintain. I've mentioned the September and May/June camping seasons where many families head out on the land, and the two weeks following the Christmas break. These periods of the year must be accommodated by the school. No amount of discussion will change this phenomenon. And why should it? The school schedule should reflect the cultural traditions of the community.

As a teacher, I aimed to make my lessons both educational and interesting. As a principal, I asked that all teachers make what was happening in their classes more attractive than many activities outside of school so students would willingly choose school instead. I did not expect teachers to become entertainers, but I did expect that extra effort would be put into meeting the needs of our unique students. Many strategies were employed to entice students to arrive on time and to remain in school and attend regularly. Physical education classes were scheduled for just after lunch or sometimes for the first period in the morning. Art would be scheduled at the end of a morning or afternoon.

We discovered that language arts and mathematics were best offered in the mornings while students were more likely to be alert. Science was often given in the afternoons. These subjects were moved around in the schedule from one term to another, one year to the next. Variety seemed to be the key, rather than any magical formula for when to offer specific courses.

We made sure that every single task attempted by the students in all courses counted for something. Participation depended on attendance so points were awarded for participation. Monthly school assemblies recognized student attendance as well as academic achievement. Month after month students were reminded that everything mattered – sportsmanship, willingness to help, an ability to read and write. Eventually they bought into it, seeing that their teachers were consistently recognizing and celebrating success. It didn't hurt that we offered small prizes for students at these assemblies.

Attendance for most of the students who started out in grade 10 in the fall of 1995 continued in the same way for the next four years. One or two moved out of town, but others moved in to take their place. Two or three left before September concluded, yet they eventually attended Arctic College for upgrading. Two boys consistently dropped out each year, usually after Christmas, only to return the following September to try again. One fellow, after turning twenty-one, was encouraged to attend a particular program at Arctic College instead. After a couple of months, he did just that.

Halfway through the grade 10 year, a decision was made to continue the grade 10 courses into the following year, finishing later at Christmas instead of June. Students needed more time to complete the requirements of their individual courses and since there were no grade 9 students poised to enter high school the following year, scheduling would be relatively simple. The DEA and the parents involved agreed that rather than rushing students through a specified program of studies, it was better to allow extra time so they could complete as many of their courses as possible and successfully earn their credits to proceed into grade 11.

By now students knew that not all of them would be automatically moved up into grade 11, as they had experienced with their K-9 schooling. They realized that secondary school required individual subject promotion and that a minimal number of credits had to be earned to proceed into grade 11. Because of the time spent "catching up," mainly in English language and mathematical skills, none of the students were set to pass many of their courses by June of that first year. Students, therefore, were relieved when asked about the possibility of extending grade 10 until Christmas of the following year. A collective weight was lifted off their shoulders and they could concentrate more on learning the material at a slower pace, rather than rushing through it.

Three students were honoured in a grade 10 graduation assembly the following January. These were the first ever grade 10 graduates of Umimmak School. To an outsider looking in, the ceremony could very well have been a grade 12 graduation, with all of the pomp and circumstance, camera flashes, nervousness, crying, wide smiles, and obvious pride shown by all. Every high school student wore a mortar hat and gown, borrowed from another school in the Baffin. The community celebrated *all* students' hard work and achievements. The three who had earned the required credits to be considered grade 11 students were especially proud in their quiet way.

When the routine of school continued, students spoke fondly of their "graduation" celebration. The fact that everyone was honoured was important. Students became more focused in their goal of graduating high school after that ceremony. Before school broke for summer, one more student had fulfilled the requirements for grade 10. Many had begun grade 11 level courses and some were well on their way towards success in those subjects. While some students continued with their grade 10 courses, others continued on the following year with grade 11 courses.

Course offerings and scheduling in general became much more complex at this time. Basically, each student's needs had to be considered individually first, and then courses were scheduled in wherever they could fit and when required. All of the combinations of grade 10 and 11 subjects had to be offered in the same classroom. As teachers, we were always offering more than one course at a time to the group. There were different expectations for assignments by the students registered in the various levels of science or English, for example. We taught the entire group when possible, then split into smaller groups every now and then. Sometimes individual work was assigned, each student progressing at their own rate.

Keeping records often became complicated but it was

absolutely essential to track each student's progress so that credits could be awarded as soon as they were earned. For example, Jeffrey finished the requirements for his grade 10 science course in the middle of February one year. Instead of automatically going on to grade 11 science, he decided he could better spend the time in class working on his other subjects in which he was falling behind. He and Susie were living in their own home and caring for their toddler son – there never seemed to be enough time for homework outside of school. Each student was given as much freedom as possible to direct their own path towards success.

With students working at so many different levels, the classroom became busier and more chaotic than before. Parts of the room had to be temporarily sectioned off for individual or small group work while the teacher addressed another group from the blackboard. Somehow, it happened because of a lot of hard work and commitment from the teachers involved. Everyone had to be creative and flexible to make the system work. The parents and the community were open to anything we wanted to try, as long as the students' well-being was at the heart of those decisions.

One year later, in September 1998, a few students began grade 12 level courses. Ten of the original students in the first grade 10 class entered school for a fourth consecutive year and three others had moved up from junior high. There were thirteen students in high school in the fall of 1998. This was the first year where there was any possibility of graduates. By the end of the year, Umimmak School did indeed produce two grade 12 graduates.

For the most part, all of the high school students actively participated in the goings-on at the school. Not all students performed well academically. A few of them had been socially promoted more than once during their elementary and junior high years. English language and mathematics skills were lacking in many of the new grade 10 students, but were abysmal for three or four of them. I also suspected solvent-abuse and fetal alcohol effects in one or two that would greatly hinder their abilities to learn. These particular students faced the enormous challenge of not only performing well in the high school environment, but also trying to catch up and then keep up with their classmates. For some this was simply not possible. All of my students were used to moving up as a group every year into each successive grade. The high school program, being based on individual subject promotion, was new to them and took a while to understand.

The large range in abilities of the grade 10 class did not take long to surface. More capable students were often paired up with the less capable ones, but different groupings for the various subject areas had to be considered. In a sense, this was not a big issue – it had to be done eventually. I knew that as grade 11 and then grade 12 courses were added to the mix in the years to come, different ability groupings would become a necessity. Reality dictated the entire high school program would take place in that one classroom, all grades at the same time; therefore, students had to learn to accept that some of their friends would race on ahead and some would be left behind.

Terry, Patrick, and Manasie were three of the most pleasant young men to have as students in a high school classroom. They were kind, polite, almost always in good humour. They began grade 10 with everyone else, yet Terry and Manasie did not earn enough credits to be considered in grade 11 until my last year in the community. Both attended school regularly; in fact, Manasie had one of the highest attendance records in the school. They had difficulty concentrating and needed to be helped along every step of the way. Mathematics in particular was extremely difficult for both of them. Homework was rarely completed. Nevertheless, Terry was known as a talented young artist in the community, and Manasie, a very capable young man out on the land. Both boys persevered and kept coming back day after day, year after year. They saw many friends move on ahead.

I was as excited as they were, the day I informed them they had completed the requirements for grade 10. The look of happiness and pride on each of their faces was priceless. They were presented with their certificates at a school assembly and awarded a gift of a watch, the face of which displayed the community name and logo. We had presented every grade 10 graduate to date with the same watch – nine or ten so far. I honestly believe that at that moment, Terry and Manasie saw that the four years they put into achieving grade 10 status was worth every single ounce of effort.

Patrick, unfortunately, was nowhere even close to entering grade 11 as I left Umimmak School. Yet, like Manasie and Terry, he attended school every day and participated in all of the classroom activities. Patrick loved music and often brought in his CDs to share with his peers. We listened to a lot of music in class – often we would study the lyrics to songs for reading and writing lessons. When asked who their best friends were on a questionnaire in a personal development course, several of the students (boys and girls) identified Patrick as one of their closest friends. He possessed qualities highly regarded by his peers. Although I am sure that he would have liked to have performed better academically, I never sensed that he felt inadequate or "less than" his classmates. He enjoyed coming to school each day. Amongst other problems, Patrick's inability to focus on school tasks contributed to his not moving up into the grade 11 level. I always marvelled at how persistent Patrick, Terry, and Manasie were, in that they never gave up and they never, ever, thought about dropping out of school.

Most students plodded along each year, gathering three and five credits for each course, and one credit every now and then for each of their CTS modules. Excitement was always in the air when the folders came out of the filing cabinet and students were allowed to colour in more squares of their "inukshuk." These files were updated two or three times a year, and only when every student in the class was able to colour in at least one square – with few exceptions, all students earned the CTS module credits. In this way, no matter how slowly for some, all students could see their achievements building.

Russell and Gayle were boyfriend and girlfriend as they entered high school. Gayle had moved to Grise Fiord from Arctic Bay to help a relative with a young child. She and Russell quickly became inseparable. Gayle decided to stay. She was very quiet and shy, and had very few close friends in town. She lived with Russell and his family. Russell and Gayle arrived at school late in

September that first year. They had been camping with Russell's family at a fiord west of the community and found themselves stranded without gasoline for more than a week. They were waiting for help so they could return to town and begin high school. When they eventually arrived back in town and showed up at school, they quickly settled into the rhythm of the class. It became evident early in the year that both of them were serious students. They showed up every day and attempted most of their homework assignments. They asked questions in class when they didn't understand something, always sitting together and helping each other when needed. They faced many obstacles along the way that would have deterred others.

In that grade 10 year, Gayle became pregnant with Russell's child and missed two full months of school. In the North, it is required that mothers-to-be fly out of the community at their eighth month of pregnancy and spend the last month within the hospital community. Both Gayle and Russell went off to Yellowknife, but not before asking for schoolwork they could do while they were away. I prepared a large binder of reading and assignments for each of them, not truly expecting they would do much, if any, of it. After the birth of their son, Gayle spent another month at home with the newborn baby. Throughout that time she completed all of the work I had given her and she was not one bit behind when she returned to class.

Russell had also managed to stay on top of his schoolwork, which not many people anticipated. He had never really liked school, and prior to grade 10 he had spent a lot of time out on the land with his father. During an early parent-teacher interview, Jaypetee, Russell's father, half-jokingly commented that he was "jealous of the school" because his son now preferred doing his homework over joining him with his dog team or out on land trips. Russell's parents were both pleasantly surprised at the change in their son's attitude towards school.

The following year, Gayle became pregnant a second time, but in true form, she managed to keep up with her schoolwork, as did Russell. Even after eventually moving out of Russell's parents' home, into their own house, they continued on with their school. Not once did either of them tell me they were considering quitting school and going to work. It was never an option they wanted to pursue. I know they sometimes struggled to keep food on the table and groceries in the refrigerator, but they kept working hard towards their high school diploma.

Russell and Gayle were those two grade 12 students in my fourth year in Grise Fiord. Much of that year they studied alone since they were the only students registered in most of their courses. They spent a lot of time in a room with me close to the office as we went over and over sample questions to prepare them for their departmental examinations in mathematics. Andrea helped them prepare for the English departmental examination. No matter how well they did in grade 12 English and math at Umimmak School, they could still be prevented from graduating if they performed poorly on those departmental exams. Each one was worth 50 percent of their final course mark.

Needless to say, both Russell and Gayle passed the examinations and became the first high school graduates at Umimmak School. It was my great privilege to see these two people complete their high school education. I could not have been more proud if they were my own children. They showed many people, more than they could possibly have imagined at the time, that small community high schools *could* work. Whether they realized it or not, these exemplary young people were inspiring role models to the youth in the community and lit the way for others to pursue a high school education. Two more students graduated with a senior secondary diploma the following year, and I have no doubt that many others followed.

6

Language is Culture

Inuktitut, the Inuit language, consists of a wide range of dialects that vary tremendously from one place to another, although residents of communities geographically close to one another have few problems communicating. Within Nunavut, vocabulary and pronunciation vary from one region to the next and can even differ between generations living in the same community. It has only been sixty years or so since most Nunavut Inuit lived in isolated camps where distinct speech patterns evolved. Many words I learned in Pangnirtung, in South Baffin, differed to those learned in Hall Beach (Melville Peninsula) and again to those heard in Grise Fiord (North Baffin). The Grise dialect was further complicated by the use of some Nunavik words – Grise Fiord was originally populated in the 1950s by Inuit forced by the federal government to relocate from northern Quebec. Modern day Nunavut sees many more Inuit moving from one settlement to another in search of work. Therefore, speakers of varying dialects often come together within the same community; however, fluent speakers generally understand each other fairly well.

Every child in Grise Fiord learns to speak Inuktitut at home long before entering kindergarten. While YoAnne and I taught at Umimmak School, Inuktitut was the first language of all students. For most of these preschoolers, their grandparents were unilingual Inuktitut speakers, possessing very little knowledge of the English language. Inuktitut is spoken in the home and within the community from the day a child is born. Children spend most of their first five years of life completely immersed in the Inuktitut language. They learn about their cultural identity through the actions, behaviours and language that they observe and hear around them each and every day. Fortunately for these children, Umimmak School has always been able to provide them with most of their schooling in their native language up to grades 5 or 6. Research suggests that reinforcing children's conceptual base in their first language throughout elementary school provides a foundation for long-term growth in English academic skills. During first-language instruction children are not just developing skills in that language, they are developing a deeper conceptual and linguistic proficiency that is strongly related to the development of literacy in a second language.

When youth enter junior high at Umimmak School, they are for all intents and purposes entering an English immersion program, taught by non-Inuit teachers. There are simply not enough trained Inuit teachers in the region, and the few Inuit educators available rarely feel confident enough to teach older students. This will change eventually, but the overwhelming majority of Inuit staff in Arctic schools work in the primary and elementary level. Outside of Grise Fiord, in most other Arctic communities, the transition from Inuktitut to English instruction begins before junior high – sometimes as early as grade 2 or 3. We were fortunate at Umimmak School in having Inuit teachers educating children in their first language, throughout the first five or six years of schooling.

Kindergarten students at the start of the year speak virtually no English whatsoever. They may utter the odd word here and there, but they have no real understanding of English. Those same children will be able to follow simple English instructions by the end of that first year. This is remarkable considering that all teaching at the K-3 level is completely in Inuktitut – there is no English in their daily structured schedule. The English that these students pick up is from what's going on in school – the informal interactions with older students and with the non-Inuit teachers. There is also the inevitable acquisition of limited English that comes about within the community as a result of watching English-language programming on television. As students progress through their early school years, the English they acquire increases in its complexity and by the time they enter grade 4 many are capable of communicating basic ideas to their non-Inuit teachers, albeit mostly in broken sentences. English words creep into their playground talk and in their various interactions outside of school. Students in the grade 4-5-6 class begin to see more English-speaking teachers on a regular basis. This is a deliberate tactic so that by the time they are about to enter grade 7 they are ready for the difficult challenge of functioning in English for most of their school day.

Anyone who has studied a second language understands the tremendous difficulties inherent in those first few days of full immersion. I completed a four-month French immersion program in New Brunswick the year before moving north and knew how difficult this sudden immersion in English would be for the students. More recently, in the spring before YoAnne and I arrived in Grise Fiord, we had attended a three-week intensive Inuktitut course offered by Nunavut Arctic College in Iqaluit. By lunch hour most days, I had a full-blown headache. At the end of each day my head simply hurt. The amount of prolonged concentration required to focus on learning this completely new language was enormous. That three-week Inuktitut course still ranks as one of the most taxing mental challenges I have ever attempted.

As students proceed through junior high, skills in English advance slowly at first, but greatly improve after the first few months. Three years later, these same students enter grade 10. Based on the amount of time needed to catch up academically with students who learn in their first language, it is not realistic to expect bilingual children to approach grade norms in English academic skills before the later grades. Inuit students have an astounding task ahead of them when they enter high school. Before graduating, they need to cover the senior secondary school curriculum (designed in Alberta and adopted by the Northwest Territories and then the Nunavut governments), earn one hundred credits and, at the very end, write standardized departmental examinations in at least two courses – English and mathematics. These exams are the same assessments written by all other grade 12 students in Nunavut, the Northwest Territories, and Alberta. The difference is that most of these other students speak English as their first language.

In 1999, 90 percent of Inuit in Nunavut spoke Inuktitut as their first language. (By 2016, that statistic had dropped to 66 percent.) Throughout their schooling lives, students went home at the end of each day to speak Inuktitut, not English. For them, English was the language of school only. Most Inuit students experienced great anxiety over and difficulty with the departmental English examination. By the time a young Inuk nears the end of grade 12, many English skills are still lacking. Some educators believe that much standardized assessment is discriminatory in its structure and disempowers minority children. The onus is on the Nunavut government to abandon these types of assessments, or to develop more culturally relevant ones. Otherwise, Inuit students in grade 12 will continue to struggle through these examinations.

Before going north, I had no formal training in teaching students learning in a second language. My strength came from an experiential environmental background, one that relied on natural science knowledge and outdoor hands-on learning. At the time, I did not fully realize how well this bent would serve me in a second language situation. I did learn many second language learning techniques along the way, but I still maintain that if logic and a lot of empathy abound, many teachers can succeed with students in a second language environment.

Nearly everything that I tried in my first few years teaching in the Baffin was a result of what I inadequately call gut instinct or, simply, common sense. I taught intuitively and relied on my innate sense of what I understood to be the right thing to do. Intuition told me that attention to the Inuktitut language and Inuit culture at all grade levels in the school, regardless of teacher competence in that language, was of great significance. I believed that a school that values Inuktitut language and Inuit culture, and conveys those ideals to its students, encourages a certain confidence and pride within those students. It seemed to me that students who were reasonably competent in their first language and proud of their cultural heritage would be more willing and able to learn in a second language.

I believed that effective teaching involved finding ways to use language, culture, and the experiences of the daily lives of students in meaningful ways in their education. While Inuktitut-speaking teachers are able to maintain the cultural connections of their young students to their families and to the greater community, teachers who do not speak the language must rely on Inuit around them and a culturally relevant school program (with an emphasis on the language) to maintain these same connections. As comfortable and competent as I grew, living in an Inuit environment, I always understood I could never assume to be capable of teaching Inuit culture to my students. I am not an Inuk. I could, however, foster an environment in which Inuit language and culture could thrive and be freely expressed.

When I became a teaching principal at Umimmak School in my second year in the community, it became my daunting responsibility to ensure that all students were provided with the best possible education. My own personal beliefs about language and culture obviously affected the overall school programming. I made it my duty to encourage the use of Inuktitut not only in my particular classroom but also in the school overall. Joanne Tompkins was a principal at Hall Beach before YoAnne and I arrived there. She had found that a conscious effort by staff to enhance the use and value of Inuktitut in the school helped to significantly strengthen Inuit perspective, language and culture. I believed in much of Joanne's philosophy of schooling.

At Umimmak School, bulletin boards and hallway displays

focused on Inuktitut first. Assemblies, school communications sent home, and radio announcements were given in Inuktitut, then, if necessary, in English. Junior and senior high students received three to five periods of Inuktitut instruction each week so that their school experience was not entirely in English. Every opportunity was taken to integrate Inuktitut into the high school program. If someone, a guest speaker for example, could speak in both languages, they were asked to use Inuktitut. It really did not matter that the teacher could not understand as they could be told about the main ideas presented to the class before or after the session. The benefits to the students of hearing a community guest speaker in their classroom using Inuktitut are far more important.

When Patrick's father, the DEA Chairperson, returned from a trip to Israel, he offered to share his experiences with the high school class. Larry had been invited to visit the Middle East because he helped an Israeli television crew in Grise Fiord the year before. Larry sat on a stool at the front of the class and began speaking in English. Immediately I asked him to please, if it was easier, speak in Inuktitut to the students. Although Larry speaks English quite well, with a smile he quickly switched over to Inuktitut. His talk went very well – students paid close attention, showing great interest. They asked many questions as he produced photographs, newspaper articles, pictures, and various souvenirs of his trip. Students were able to express themselves in Inuktitut without difficulty or hesitation. It makes sense to me that the story of an Inuk in Israel should be told from the Inuk's perspective and in the Inuit language. In having Larry tell his story in Inuktitut, students implicitly learned that Inuktitut was as valuable and as important as English in their high school lives.

Today, decades later, my heart warms when I hear Inuktitut being spoken. Thanks to social media and the Internet, and an increased interest in the Far North, there are many opportunities to hear this beautiful language. Upon hearing the words and familiar voices I am immediately taken back to those wonderful years in the Baffin.

7

Culturally Relevant Curriculum and
Land-Based Teaching

In 1989, the year that YoAnne and I first arrived in the Baffin, school board supervisors and consultants were travelling from community to community presenting workshops on *Piniaqtavut*. This was a new initiative, an integrated program designed to meet the cultural, linguistic and academic needs of Baffin students. The *Piniaqtavut* program provided culturally relevant, high-interest themes for students in kindergarten through grade 9. *Piniaqtavut* encouraged a whole language, theme-based approach to teaching. One school of thought suggests that whole language legitimizes the way Indigenous people generally perceive learning. Learning should be based in the real world and real language must be part of it. That is, learning should relate to living in a holistic and relevant way.

In theme-based programs, students explore a concept through many lenses. Subject areas such as language arts, science, health, mathematics, and social studies are integrated into predetermined grade-appropriate themes. For example, at the grade 2 level, a recommended core unit entitled "Polar Bears" would not only encompass extensive reading and writing about them, but students would also learn about the biology of polar bears and their impact on Inuit society. Art projects would focus on the polar bear, as would a number of math activities. A well-defined theme-based program allows students to connect ideas, concepts, and experiences. Building bridges across content areas also gives students a context in which to apply their acquired skills.

Joanne Tompkins led the way in the Baffin with "theming and teaming" at her school. She found that theming provided the staff with a forum to look critically at how the program was put together, and it provided an opportunity for them to work as a team. She saw that teaming helped people to come out of their classrooms and see the bigger picture of the school program and the responsibility to contribute to the total school program. News of Joanne's success with theme teaching and team collaborations spread throughout the region and many other schools attempted similar strategies. Even though it took a lot of time to produce teaching resources to support the individual thematic units, Inuit teachers embraced *Piniaqtavut*.

By the time YoAnne and I reached Grise Fiord in 1995, *Piniaqtavut* was fairly well established in all Baffin schools. We had seen the program in action in Pangnirtung and Hall Beach and we believed in its merits. Students at all grade levels loved learning the *Piniaqtavut* themes – they were purposeful, interesting and meaningful to students living in the North. As a high school teacher I had been involved mostly with the senior secondary curriculum, a southern-based curriculum far removed from the ideals of *Piniaqtavut*. For me, going to Grise Fiord was not only an opportunity to start up a brand-new high school program, it was also a chance to connect that new senior high program more seamlessly to the already existing, and more culturally relevant, K-9 *Piniaqtavut* program.

We arrived at Umimmak School at just the right moment. The new K-12 curriculum from the Inuit perspective, *Inuuqatigiit*, was about to be implemented in all Nunavut schools. Unlike *Piniaqtavut*, which is a program, *Inuuqatigiit* is a curriculum document. The foundation for *Inuuqatigiit* comes from Inuit philosophy. It focuses on the enhancement and enrichment of the language and culture of Inuit students and promotes integration of the Inuit perspective with the standard school curriculum.

The notion of cultural relevance moves beyond language to include other aspects of student and school culture. Inuit students learning in a typical Western-European styled school system do not see their culture, background or history represented in their textbooks or program of studies. What they may see is a distorted version of that culture, background or history. They may also notice certain staffing patterns in school. As an example, the junior and senior high school teachers, the principal, and the vast majority of the visiting school board officials to Umimmak School were all non-Inuit. The primary teachers, custodian and office staff were Inuit. What might this observation tell young Inuit students?

Culturally relevant teaching empowers students by using cultural examples to impart knowledge, skills, and attitudes. The implementation of *Inuuqatigiit* meant that even more senior secondary programs would be given much needed injections of Inuit culture. The best high school teachers throughout the North had been substituting northern, more culturally relevant materials into the curriculum all along the way – for them, *Inuuqatigiit* was not a new concept. Holding the physical curriculum document in their hands, however, meant that many other teachers would be expected to do the same thing in their classrooms as well. A more structured support network focusing on Inuit culture in the curriculum for senior high teachers was very much welcome.

In the spring before we made the move to Grise Fiord, I had become involved in the new Nunavut High Schools Project (NHSP). As a member of the science committee, I was involved in the integrating of academic and general level science curriculums. This was to aid new teachers in the North faced with the very real possibility of having to teach two different levels of science at the same time within one classroom. In adjusting the curriculum, attention to *Inuuqatigiit* was foremost in our minds. Eventually, the science committee developed several culturally relevant components to the curriculum, for example the *Science of the Qulliit* (seal oil lamp) and the *Science of Igunaq* (aged walrus meat). I later became heavily involved in the NHSP art committee, where an Inuit art curriculum was to be developed that embraced all Inuit art forms. The NHSP's English and social studies committees eventually produced humanities materials as well. All of this work served to support senior secondary teachers throughout the Baffin and the rest of Nunavut with relevant teaching ideas for their Inuit students more so than ever before.

Over the years, as I developed lessons for my students and programming for the school, I made a sincere attempt to follow the *Inuuqatigiit* philosophy, integrating traditional Inuit values and beliefs with the school program so that each day was as meaningful as possible for students. I found that the entire staff at Umimmak School shared the same conviction and worked very well together. When new non-Inuit teachers arrived, they were encouraged to teach culturally relevant topics to their students and were given support from other staff and community members. They were also asked to learn a small amount of Inuktitut from their students. This communicates a great deal of respect to students and Inuit teachers. Even simple gestures boost the status of the students' first language within the school setting and promote increased motivation to learn both English and Inuktitut.

In my first fall teaching the new grade 10 class in Grise Fiord, one of my subjects was a northern studies course. The curriculum was quite vague – I was told to teach what I thought best. We did a lot of mapping, northern history and governance, but by far the most engaging unit was the story of the High Arctic Exiles. I was warned that it might be a volatile topic. Grise Fiord is one of several "exiled" communities. It was settled by Inuit who, in the 1950s, were forced by the federal government to leave their home in Arctic Quebec to serve as human flagpoles and assert Canadian sovereignty in the High Arctic. Many families were split up in the process. Life for these displaced Inuit was exceptionally difficult for many years. Many did not survive. Only a few of the original "exiles" still lived in the community, but many of their children and families continued to make Grise their home. Over time, Inuit from other communities had moved in, adding to the mix of peoples in the hamlet. Some families sympathized with the exiles and some did not. The story is complicated by the fact that in the mid 1990s the federal government awarded compensation to people for the tragedy. This action proved a bit controversial within the community as many people did not completely agree with the choice of which residents should receive the compensation.

My grade 10 class consisted of children from all Grise Fiord families. I had to be impartial and let everyone have their say. Truth be known, at that time I knew very little about the details of the story. I learned about it as I facilitated the class discussion. Exploring the many sides of the High Arctic Exiles story turned out to be an enlightening experience for me as well as my students. I did not teach them anything – I only directed the daily lessons.

The National Film Board had recently produced the documentary *Broken Promises*, which spoke of the events from the perspective of the Inuit themselves. We watched the film together. Guest speakers from within the community gave their own personal perspectives to the class. Students were encouraged to write about the topic and to join in on class discussions. They were polite and respectful of the points of view of their classmates.

There was no political fallout in the community as a result of these sensitive discussions at the school. Most residents sat back and observed from a distance. I think the parents and other adults in town wanted their children to hear all sides of the story so they could make up their own minds. As for culturally relevant and meaningful lessons, I don't think I could have chosen a better topic for a grade 10 northern studies course at Umimmak School. I was very pleased with the way it turned out.

Every teacher at Umimmak School substituted parts of the curriculum at different times with their own units so that more meaningful learning could occur in their classrooms. YoAnne spent three weeks with her multilevel junior high class researching traditional Inuit games, constructing a few of the props required for those games, and then co-ordinating a school-wide Inuit games afternoon. All students, and their parents, were challenged at the one-foot-high kick, muskox fight, airplane, mouth pull, ear pull, bench reach, kneel jump, and a variety of others. The athleticism required to execute these deceptively simple movements is significant.

Two games, *ajagaak* and *nugluktuq*, proved to be quite popular. In *ajagaak*, an eight-inch string is attached to any animal bone with one or more holes in it. The other end of the string is attached to a small bone tip. The object of the game is to hold the bone tip in one hand and swing the bone into the air trying to spear the bone with the bone tip. Inuktitut songs were sung as the game progressed and children cheered for one another as the bone was swung repeatedly into the air. For *nugluktuq*, a spindle-shaped piece of caribou antler with holes drilled through it is hung from the ceiling at shoulder height. Players form a circle around it and, using spears narrow enough to fit into the drilled holes, each player tries to spear one of the holes. As everyone plays at the same time, it becomes quite chaotic. Action stops only when someone slides their spear into a hole. This counts as one point and then the play continues.

Students love all games, but by involving them in creating materials and then organizing an event where their parents could join in, YoAnne celebrated their heritage at the same time.

YoAnne and I were not the only non-Inuit teachers in Grise Fiord. Harry was in the community for two years before heading home to Prince Edward Island. Andrea, Tammy, Vincent, Cory, Krista, and Stephen came from Ontario, Nova Scotia, and Newfoundland throughout the four years we were there. Each one of them brought enthusiasm and new ideas to the school program. With the help of Mimi, Mary, Jane (who became the primary teacher when Mary went on leave to complete her education degree), and so many other Inuit in town, all of we *qallunaat* learned to incorporate many culturally relevant themes into our teaching. The spirit of *Inuuqatigiit* was certainly alive and well at Umimmak School.

To help address the challenge of making *Inuuqatigiit* work, money was put aside in the budget each year for the hiring of local cultural instructors to deliver important traditional teaching in Inuktitut. Wherever possible, any third-party funding that could be secured was also put towards traditional teachings. Mary's mother-in-law, Rynee, worked at the school every year that we lived in Grise. She taught countless young Inuit how to prepare seal and caribou skins for sewing and how to make duffel socks and mittens.

I had a Polaroid snapshot tacked to the wall directly in front of my work table at home. YoAnne and I are standing on either side of a short, round, elderly women. We are all wearing dark sunglasses to shade our eyes from the bright sunlight. I have my left arm over the woman's shoulder and YoAnne is hunched over, leaning in towards the woman, her face pressed against the woman's cheek. Sadly, I have long since lost this photo. Rynee had asked her granddaughter to take the photo for us at the airstrip as we left town for the very last time. Adeline snapped one off for Rynee too. In the hallway at school, earlier in the week, this beautiful sweet lady had taken us aside, placed her hands on both of our arms and, struggling with her English words and smiling, she said, "Don't go ... stay!" We were so touched by this simple gesture of friendship. All we could do was smile back at her and give her a hug. Whenever I think of cultural inclusion in the school program, I always imagine Rynee's smiling face first.

Rynee was especially good at working with sealskins. Often she would bring in several dried skins and have young students practise softening the pelts. Recently dried skins are extremely stiff and difficult to work with as they retain the flat, scalloped-edged shape that develops as they are stretched tightly over a wooden frame with sinew and left to dry outside in the Arctic air. Students could spend the better half of their weekly cultural skills classes to soften just one pelt. String is very loosely sewn around the edge of the skin and then pulled together like a purse string. By holding the string up around shoulder height, you then stomp all over the skin, gradually softening it enough to be stitched into *kamiks* (boots) or mitts or any other required piece of clothing. What a sight to behold as eight young Inuit boys and girls stomp briskly over their sealskins, chatting and laughing as they proceed.

Pijamini, Mimi and Geela's father, the Elder we had met on that first flight into town, had worked at the school for years but he stayed on as a cultural instructor only for that first year I was at Umimmak School. Pijamini was a born teacher. He was knowledgeable in so many cultural traditions – he would tell personal hunting stories and legends, give demonstrations on how to cut up meat, and teach students how to carve in soapstone. Pijamini would sometimes act as a guide and go on the land with students of any age.

I remember him speaking to the junior high class about navigating by the stars in wintertime. He spoke in Inuktitut as he pointed out the various constellations on a massive glow-in-the-dark star chart that we had ordered for the school. Every now and then, he would ask a student to turn out the lights and the whole class would *ooh* and *aah* in wonder at the glowing stars before their eyes. They learned all of the Inuktitut names for the constellations as well as the Inuit origins of the stories behind them. If a *qallunaaq* had taught that particular lesson, the students would have learned about the Big Dipper and Cassiopeia instead of *Tukturjuit* (caribou) and *Ursuutaattiaq* (sealskin blubber container).

One advantage of the long dark season in the High Arctic is that you can take students out in the middle of the day to star watch, and that's exactly how Pijamini ended his session on navigating by the stars. Off the group went, clothed in parkas and heavy boots, to the shoreline in front of the school. For half an hour or so all heads were cranked back searching out the constellations they had just learned about from a knowledgeable Elder.

Pijamini gave the students in kindergarten through grade 9 a biology lesson through a partial walrus dissection. Everyone crammed into YoAnne's junior high classroom. Students had already participated in the ptarmigan dissection the day before and were told that after the walrus they would also dissect a seal and then a fish. Traditionally, Inuit children were first encouraged to watch and observe adults at their tasks in order to learn; later they would practise doing those tasks as adults instructed them. In his quiet, patient way, Pijamini commanded respect – he always had the full attention of the students. His demonstrations followed the traditional ways of teaching children. We have video footage of his walrus dissection, so I am able to describe the activity in detail.

Pijamini sat on the floor next to a large disembodied walrus head that was so big it barely fit inside a large plastic green garbage bag. Brown butcher's paper was placed under the plastic to save the classroom rug from any bloody spills. Pijamini's tools – a long heavy knife, a smaller one, and a large roasting fork from the school's kitchen – were laid out on the floor by his side. Forty students and three teachers sat at desks or on the edge of tables or stretched out on the floor as close as possible to the action.

Pijamini invited Levi, a tall, well-built, grade 9 student who was already a skilled outdoorsman, to show the class how to turn a walrus whisker into a ring. Levi quickly plucked out a thick, translucent whisker from the walrus head and with a smile deftly manipulated the tapered hollow tube into a perfectly round ring. All the while, Pijamini spoke in Inuktitut. He made a ring for himself and then allowed ten to fifteen of the students closest to him to do the same. Much talking and laughing ensued as children tried to make their own rings. Many were successful.

Pijamini took his utility knife and very carefully sliced into the skin of the walrus just below the nose. He spoke constantly, asking questions and waiting for responses as he continued with his work. The walrus had two sixteen-inch long creamy white tusks protruding from its upper jaw. He tapped on the tusks then pointed to several carved ivory dogsled toggles he had brought with him, indicating they were made from the tusks of a walrus.

Pijamini then sliced off the whiskers and underlying flesh, revealing a mass of fatty material under the skin. As he continued, he asked for the names of the various parts. They responded well, sometimes answering in unison. Using his larger knife, he cut away the firm white blubbery parts of the head. He dug in deep and cut out a large piece of cartilage from somewhere within the walrus head. Speaking as he carved away at the lump in his hand, he soon produced a perfectly round ball-shaped object. He told Alex to throw the ball as hard as he could onto the floor. When Alex did this, the ball bounced hard off the floor, hit the ceiling and bounced again on the floor. The crowd was amazed. *Oooh! Aaah!*

Pijamini had Mosha carve another ball by himself. As he finished, Mosha handed it to Rhoda, who immediately bounced it hard off the floor. Jimmy ducked as Rhoda wound up. Students laughed louder and louder. Over in the corner, Frankie was concentrating on balancing a walrus whisker on his curled upper lip, trying to make a whisker into a moustache. After realizing he had been noticed by his classmates, he laughed and dropped the whisker.

As all of this was going on, Pijamini began to tell walrus stories. He was animated in his storytelling, smiling and gesturing often. Many students asked questions throughout the stories. Without any instruction from him, they placed all of the cartilage "superballs" in a plastic water-filled container at his side. He sharpened his knife and continued with the dissection, cutting into the lip of the animal. Students were very close to him on the floor but he did not ask them to move back. As he spoke, he pointed to parts of the walrus with his knife, sometimes making a gentle, stabbing motion. He took care as he dissected out one of the eyeballs. He displayed the intact eye to the group, piercing it so all of the fluid ran out and retrieving the lens of the eye to show them. More *ooohs* and *aaahs*!

Pijamini again asked for Mosha's help. Mosha placed his hand inside the mouth of the walrus, feeling around for something, but it took too long to find what he was looking for. Pijamini then motioned for Jimmy to try. After a bit of a struggle, the ten-inch long tongue of the walrus was revealed. As Pijamini removed it and showed the group, everyone stuck out their own tongues and laughed.

By this time, the demonstration had been going on for close to an hour. YoAnne returned to the classroom carrying a plate and a large covered aluminum pot, which she set on the floor beside Pijamini. He removed the foil to reveal big chunks of cooked steaming walrus meat in a thick broth, then cut up the chunks and distributed them to students. An appropriate ending to an interesting, certainly meaningful, lesson.

Annie (Pijamini's wife), Martha, Minnie, Imooshie, and countless others helped in the traditional teachings at the school. The homeroom teacher stayed with the group for the weekly sessions, to take care of any classroom management issues that may have arisen, leaving the local instructors to deal only with the teaching of the traditional skill. Not surprisingly, however, very few discipline problems occurred during these particular classes. Almost all cultural instructors were unilingual Inuktitut speakers and conducted their classes in Inuktitut and, consciously or not, they taught students new Inuktitut words constantly.

In Hall Beach, some of the cultural skills classes were turned into a game where students were fined a nominal fee of five cents or so if an English word crept into the conversation. If an Inuktitut word was not known, the object or idea to be named was to be described in other Inuktitut words so that the group could discover the new word together. With my limited vocabulary, anytime I participated in this challenge I had to resort to charades – but I did learn more Inuktitut.

Throughout any cultural activities, Elders were encouraged to share their personal histories and stories with the children. Sometimes songs were sung and legends were told as groups of students worked away on a project.

Each week, Inuit staff planned with the cultural instructors so that cultural information linked to the predetermined thematic units was shared and integrated into lessons for all grade levels. This information was also shared with non-Inuit staff at other weekly theme-planning sessions. Whenever possible, other local resource people were hired to deliver lessons on specific traditional knowledge or skills and encouraged to speak to students in Inuktitut. For example, prior to the polar bear hunt the Renewable Resource Officer spoke about local polar bear quotas and how they were determined; an Elder discussed traditional ways of predicting the weather; seal hunting tactics were always popular.

The importance of having Elders and other community members instructing students in traditional values and skills, in the Inuktitut language, at school on a regular basis cannot be overstated. Parental involvement is one way in which community values, lifestyles, and realities can affect the school; parents in the school ensure that their language and culture, and the expectations they have for their children, are heard and made a priority.

I have come to understand that language and culture cannot be separated. The language that children bring to school inevitably affects how and what they learn. So much of a person's culture is expressed in the use of certain words. Many words in one language cannot be translated into another. It would be very difficult to teach Inuit children all of the different types of snow and ice in any other language but Inuktitut – there are numerous Inuktitut words describing snow and many more for ice. By encouraging students of all ages to participate in activities facilitated by respected community members, given in their own language, students develop invaluable knowledge as well as self-confidence and pride in their cultural heritage.

At a meeting in the school during the fall, a parent commented that no matter how well a student succeeds in the modern school system, Inuit still need to learn traditional skills and to develop respect for living things and the environment. Inuit will always hunt and need to survive on the land. The parent explained the Arctic land, water, and sky would always be part of Inuit culture, far into the future, and the school had to offer opportunities for their children to learn important land skills. People were emphatic in letting the school know that the knowledge of the Elders and the traditionally skilled people in town must be passed on to students through activities at the school, as well as at home and within the community.

The community was consulted regularly for ideas and anyone who was available to help teach an activity was quickly scheduled in. The Elders, with the help of school staff, were encouraged to organize most of their own activities themselves, in school as well as out on the land. They were given as much freedom as possible within the school program. One year, Mimi went to a Hunters and Trappers Organization meeting, armed with a list of student-generated activity ideas. At its end, she had a long list of names of men and women who would take the students out over the next few months for traditional activities. Community members hired to teach cultural skills provided as much of their own materials as they could. This included snowmobiles, *qamouti*, camp stoves, pots and pans, bowls and cups for land excursions, skins, knives, specialized carving tools, and so on. A conscious attempt was made to share community resources. Much stone, ivory, scrap lumber, and plywood was generously donated to the school for student use.

A wide variety of land-based activities was offered to students throughout the years we lived in Grise Fiord: how to build snow shelters and igloos; how to light a *qulliq* (seal oil lamp) and to maintain its flame; how to pack a *qamoutik* (sled); how to command and lead a dog team; how to locate animals for the hunt; skinning techniques for ptarmigan, seal, caribou, polar bear, and muskox; how to predict weather and read the stars, and where to find fresh drinking water; how to use a Coleman stove and how to prepare boxes of food for camping trips; how to smoke meat; how to cook simple meals while camping; how to make canvas tents, *ulus* (women's knives), and harpoons; and more.

One year, Robert, an ex-military man, moved back to town with his Inuk wife and family, and within weeks he was offering a four-day GPS workshop to senior students. Many hunters were using this technology and students wanted to know more about it. During that workshop, students learned more pertinent geometry, trigonometry, and geography than I could have taught them in a month of Earth science and mathematics classes.

As a former interpretive naturalist, I have a deep love and respect for the natural environment. I understand how first-hand experience in seeing, touching, smelling, and hearing the world around us allows all of us to learn in a much more fundamental, meaningful way than in any other learning situation. Natural settings provide a context for teaching and learning that textbook or computer-based learning environments can't compete with. When students learn in outdoor settings as compared to staying in the classroom, they learn more quickly, appreciate the experience more, and retain skills and knowledge much longer. For many Inuit youth, already raised in an outdoor lifestyle, land-based, experiential education is the most fitting environment in which to learn.

Land-based activities at Umimmak School became the soul of the school program. Whether it was softening skins in a classroom, or fashioning a harpoon head from scrap aluminum at the Hamlet garage, or spending an afternoon searching for Arctic hare, or camping for a week on Devon Island, the land-based activities helped bridge the gap between the school program and the community. For kindergarten through grade 9, all of the important components of the school program fell into place around these land themes. Language arts, social studies, science, health, and mathematics (to a lesser extent) were learned as integrated components of larger themes. And, although the schedules for senior high students were still divided into separate subject areas (mostly for administrative purposes), interdisciplinary teaching according to themes in grades 10, 11, and 12 was greatly encouraged.

Considerable attention was paid to Inuktitut language and Inuit culture within the school program. This focus on land-based education reflected a genuine respect for Inuit and their lives, and in my experience helped encourage students and their families to develop an even stronger cultural pride and identity within the school context.

8

Art in the Inuit Classroom

A discussion of language, culture, and culturally relevant curriculum in Inuit schools must include the importance of art education in the school program. Many Indigenous students exhibit considerable artistic talent. I have always been truly impressed by the quality of artwork produced in northern classrooms.

Being artistically inclined myself, I was happy to take on the additional responsibility of developing an art program in Pangnirtung when I first arrived in the North as a high school science teacher. We drew, we painted, we carved, we tried lino block and silk screen printing. Walls in the old school were covered in colourful murals. We even visited the local tapestry studio on a regular basis to learn how to weave. I enjoyed teaching art so much that I gladly took on any art teaching I could, both in Hall Beach and later in Grise Fiord.

I became a member of the Nunavut High School Project Art committee and participated in the development of a draft Nunavut art curriculum for senior high school. In previous years, the only official senior high art curriculum that teachers had as a guideline came from Alberta. In the early to mid 1990s, the Saskatchewan K-9 art curriculum was adopted as an additional resource. However, neither of these curriculum documents highlighted Inuit art to any extent, and local arts traditions were given no importance in the program at all. In 1999, when YoAnne and I left the North, a comprehensive Nunavut arts curriculum still had not been completed.

In a sense, I was lucky to not have been tied to any particular program of studies for art. In the absence of a culturally relevant art curriculum, teachers were encouraged to be creative and to start with what the students and the community were already interested in. I drew on my personal strengths as an artist, looked to the community for types of art forms familiar to the students, and asked for help from local craftspeople in the delivery of the program. Colleagues on staff were helpful as well and occasionally contributed to the program.

Inuit possess a long cultural history of artistic expression – art has been produced in Arctic Canada for the last 4,000 years. Inuit have always made functional clothing, shelters, utensils, tools, and weapons using materials offered by the natural world. The chipped flint tools and weapon points that have been discovered over the years are very well made – some say, an art form. It is evident that the people who crafted these pieces were interested in more than just the functional aspects of stone tools as they were often fashioned into highly artistic forms. Multi-coloured flints, for example, were chipped evenly and symmetrically, often with decorative edge serrations. The skill required for the crafting of such pleasing forms carries on today in Inuit communities. Inuit place great value in an aptitude for creative expression. Hands that once carved snow knives and harpoon tips, now shape bone, ivory, antler, and soapstone carvings; fingers that once stitched clothing to guard against the cold Arctic weather, now also weave woollen tapestries and sew appliqué.

It didn't take long for me to discover that some of my senior students at Umimmak School were already accomplished artists and well regarded in the community for their talents. Artistic youth receive a great deal of praise from their peers, family and community. If, for example, someone wanted a line drawing of a polar bear, they knew to ask Terry. He was always happy to comply, and in very little time he would produce a well-proportioned, realistic illustration of the animal. Terry struggled in the core academic subjects in school, yet he was known amongst his classmates as "a real artist." Two years in a row he won an annual national art competition where his work appeared in a student art calendar. He was honoured for this achievement in many ways by his friends and family, as well as at the school.

As an educator, I observed the tangible link between a student's success in the art program and their feelings of self-esteem and cultural identity. Much of what students choose to capture in their art is a direct reflection of their own culture. Even the youngest of students draw seal hunters, snowmobiles, whales, and birds. As a person who has been interested in art since childhood, I have an emotional understanding of how I am affected when I draw and paint and when I receive praise for my work. On many levels, I know that part of my sense of self is owed to my identity and success as an artist. It makes sense to me that art is a powerful tool for enhancing self-esteem and improving the self-concept of students in the classroom.

Educators agree that an arts education is valuable. Defined widely, arts education includes the fine arts (visual) and the performing arts (music and drama). None of the schools in which I taught in the North had any music or drama classes, but they all offered drawing, painting, carving, printmaking, sewing, and a number of other visual art activities. Many students were very interested in music but the schools simply did not have the budget for purchasing instruments, nor the trained staff to deliver the program. Any music education occurred at home and within the community. Several of my students did play guitar, drums, and keyboard. Many of their family members sang and played a variety of instruments, which of course was greatly appreciated at the many community celebrations throughout the year.

In Grise Fiord, I learned that none of my students had received any structured art lessons in school. Except for the usual art components that accompany student projects at the primary and elementary level, my grade 10 class had no experience with formalized art teaching. Because I taught most subjects all day with the same students I had the flexibility of changing the schedule to suit our daily needs. Art was a three-credit course and was scheduled in for roughly four forty-five-minute periods a week, yet often that changed to double periods in one day in order to finish particular projects. Every student had a relative who carved or sewed or drew or was artistic in some recognizable way. The students had more real-life background in "art" than many southern students of the same age. Even though many of them were budding artists-in-the-rough, we began the year with a unit on the fundamentals, drawing and painting, colour theory, and the like. It was a large unit since most topics were completely new to the students. However, the time spent on these basics was of great interest to them and worthwhile in the long run. No matter how sophisticated their art became in the future, and no matter what medium they chose to work with, a solid background in the fundamentals of art would be useful.

Students were keenly interested in everything from learning the different grades of pencils, to working with charcoal, conté, and pastels, to pen and ink drawing. They enjoyed art class a great deal. At the same time, they were very serious, concentrating on learning all the techniques. We explored line and texture, design and composition. We set up three-dimensional geometric shapes on a central table with strong lighting to learn about the properties of light and shade. Still-life compositions were arranged in the classroom for students to practise. With prodding, most students eventually took turns acting as models, climbing up on top of that central table for their classmates when the life drawing section of the course began. Everyone was encouraged to show their work and each and every piece of artwork produced was signed and stored in a handmade Bristol board portfolio at the back of the classroom.

They progressed quickly from the basics of line and composition and went on to experiment in various types of printmaking, carving and sculpture, skin preparation, pattern making and sewing, tool and jewelry making, and even construction technology, computer-assisted art, and videography. Many diverse units were offered to students over the years. Interestingly enough, whatever the senior students were doing in art at the school often trickled down into the junior high class as well as the elementary and primary classes. Sometimes older students went into the younger classes to help present an art activity with the teacher.

Much research focuses on the importance of arts education in improving academic achievement (increased competency in math, for example). However, arts education in itself has great value too. It is said to encourage the development of planning and listening skills, creative thinking, concentration, and co-operative learning, and to improve emotional intelligence. It helps in the understanding of spatial relationships and enhances hand-eye coordination. An arts education can encourage multicultural appreciation. The art teacher's first priority is to build self-confidence in students as well as an interest in and concern for the visual world.

When my students first began drawing life figures, only one or two of the bravest would get up on that table and model for their peers. Aside from the fact that it was difficult to sit or stand in one position for any length of time, it was especially hard to be the centre of attention and to be looked at so intensely for such a long time. Many Inuit shy away from being in the spotlight in most situations – it is not a cultural practise to make yourself the focus of attention. It was a slow process, but constant encouragement and a desire to see drawings of themselves gave students the courage to model for their classmates. Near the end of the unit, I had so many volunteers that I had to select the models from all the raised hands.

Students risk a great deal in attempting to draw something they have never drawn before, or to use colours in new ways, or to carve into an unknown material for the first time. The creating of art is also a very personal endeavour. In a sense, students are opening themselves up for the world to see. I continually praised their work at every step along the way. Normally quiet students, who fade into the background at school, often produce the most interesting artwork. Andrew rarely spoke in class; even amongst his friends he was considered "the quiet one." Yet when he drew, he exhibited a sense of humour that surprised everyone. Not only was the subject of his art often comical, he laughed a lot with students as they critiqued his work. While participation in art is mostly a solitary activity, after the work is complete, it is viewed by many. Lymieky liked to give the impression he didn't care much about anything at school, yet he discovered he was a talented watercolourist and took great pride in his work. He shyly accepted praise from his classmates, with a telling grin.

The environment of the art studio lends itself to students experimenting with ideas and self-discovery. Although I had a wonderful studio for the art program in Pangnirtung (a large, well-lit portable classroom with a loft, completely separated from the school), in Grise Fiord my homeroom classroom was all we had. However, I certainly observed students in the studio atmosphere of art class behaving quite differently as compared to their behaviours in that same classroom during math or English. When it came time for art class, tables and chairs were moved and rearranged, music was played, and the lighting was adjusted. Students moved about much more freely, and the room hummed with all the discussions amongst students.

In this relaxed environment they took more risks, they ventured further with their work, they experimented more loosely. If something didn't work out the way they had envisioned, they would simply try again. They felt secure and comfortable in this atmosphere. I would often sit at the back of the room and watch with great pleasure as they went about creating their work. When art class was over, tables and chairs would be moved back into place, the music would be turned off, and a different ambience would permeate that very same space.

Not only does arts education help with positive self-esteem, it is now recognized for its capacity to enable students to express emotions, perhaps even as therapy in the healing of physical or emotional trauma. Arts education develops trust, self-acceptance, and acceptance of others. Research shows students with education in the arts make more emotionally literate decisions and are more aware of their feelings and of the feelings of those around them. Many times, I listened in on my students' chatter throughout the art period. It was not evesdropping – most of the time they spoke to one another in Inuktitut and my limited facility with the language guarded their privacy. But the ease and comfort with which they spoke to one another, often not specifically about the task at hand, warmed my heart. I felt lucky to be there.

I remember a particular discussion that arose in my classroom of Inuit teenagers after I asked them to do two abstract paintings – one portraying happiness and one portraying sadness. I was expecting dumbfounded expressions, yet to my surprise they began chatting at once to each other about their happy and sad experiences. There were enough English words sprinkled about that I understood they were not simply humouring me. They took the task very seriously. Soon they began relating their feelings to colours – dark brooding colours to represent gloom and sadness, and bright cheery colours for happiness. Some thought about textures and quality of lines. All the while they put paint to paper, small groups of students engaged in separate conversations about the topics of their paintings.

I found my senior students also enjoyed short, experimental activities in art. I thought it would be interesting to play a little with brain theory in art. I am, after all, a student of science as well. I had tried these techniques myself, years earlier, after discovering Betty Edwards' *Drawing on the Right Side of the Brain*. She suggested that practical applications of brain theory in the enhancing of creativity and artistic confidence involves so-called "right-brain" activities. To summarize simply, the dominant left side of the brain is responsible for verbal, symbolic, logical, and analytical thought, so the "left-brain" processes information on linear, sequential data; the subdominant right side of the brain is responsible for visual, spatial, relational, holistic, and perceptual thinking, so the right-brain uses intuition, and experiences leaps of insight. In order to gain access to the creative right-brain, we must present the brain with a job that the left-brain will turn down. By learning how to purposely access the right-brain, we gain access to brain functions that are often obscured by language.

As an exercise designed to stimulate right-brain thinking, I asked students to first draw a profile of a person's head on the left side of a piece of paper, with the head facing in towards the centre of the page. They were then instructed to draw two horizontal lines one at the top of the profile and another at the bottom. They soon guessed at this stage that I was going to ask them to complete the "vase." But first, I asked that they go back over the drawing of the profile with a pencil, naming each part of the face as they got to it. This is a left-brain task – naming symbolic shapes. Students were asked to repeat this a second time and then told to draw the profile in reverse, in effect, completing the vase. They were instructed to be sure that the vase was as symmetrical as possible.

As students drew the second profile, they all showed visible signs of mental conflict. They began to giggle at themselves as they unintentionally drew lines in the opposite direction to what they really wanted. So, without further instruction, they began to scan back and forth between the two profiles, estimating angles, curves, and length of lines in relation to the opposite shapes. They were no longer drawing a profile or finishing the vase. The task had become nameless. The students had made the shift from left-brain to right-brain function. Rather than thinking about the face part that they needed to draw next, they were using the shape of the space between the two profiles as their guide.

Students always responded well as I tried other right-brain exercises throughout the year as "art aerobics" or warm-ups for other art activities. They especially liked learning how to forge a signature by turning it upside down before copying – this always elicited exclamations of wonder.

Every culture has its own unique way of expressing itself artistically. Art remains a fundamental aspect of everyday life in the North today. The non-verbal expressive nature of art is a link for

Inuit to a rich heritage. Often Inuit art portrays the animals and people of the Arctic world. Sometimes mythical figures are depicted or creatures from the artist's imagination. Many of my students were keen on learning how to carve. Soapstone carvings are produced by Inuit in all Arctic communities – the most well-known Inuit artists are carvers of stone. I felt silly showing Inuit how to work stone, so I asked the father of two elementary students to teach carving techniques to the senior art class.

Lootie was happy to be asked and came in for two hours each day for a week. In addition to working part-time for the Hamlet, he was an accomplished artist and earned a portion of his living through the selling of his carvings and metal jewelry. Lootie had taught jewelry-making techniques to adults at an Arctic College campus in a larger community and was also preparing for an Indigenous Art Show in Arizona for the following spring. Prior to him arriving, each student had mixed and poured plaster of Paris and vermiculite into milk cartons of various shapes and sizes. By the time of the first class, the plaster mixture had hardened and was ready to carve. The cardboard carton was peeled off each block of plaster. Students brought in their own carving knives for the project. They could hardly wait to begin.

I was quite delighted to see Lootie walking from student to student, monitoring the progress of each one as he instructed them on the correct proportioning of the human face. He said most of them could probably carve an animal reasonably well but the facial features of a person were very difficult to do. This is why he chose to teach the class how to carve a face. Lootie carved his own piece of plaster only occasionally when the students were ready to go on to a different part of the work. Most of his time was spent guiding the class in the step-by-step process of producing the likeness of a face out of the plaster. Lootie spoke entirely in Inuktitut as he taught these eager students, using English words only when the appropriate Inuktitut word would not come soon enough. He was attentive to each student and demonstrated immense patience. He was not afraid to be critical of their work, offering ways to change or improve on their progress. However, Lootie would not carve any student's piece for them – they had to do it themselves.

Throughout the week he spoke not only of the specific task at hand but also of his experiences as a working artist, of hunting and travelling over the land, of family and community life, and about many other topics. As each day passed, the rectangular blocks of plaster were slowly and magically transformed into a collection of animated faces, each one reflecting a unique artistic style. By Friday, students were truly amazed at what they had accomplished. And from a cultural perspective, they learned far more than the simple proportions of a face.

Inuit society is so rich in culture that it would be easy to focus almost exclusively on the North and its people. There is, however, a serious attempt made by schools to adopt themes throughout the year that allow teachers and students to learn about the world at large too. Most schools, for example, explore a "multiculturalism" theme at some time during the school year. Art activities for the teaching of this integrated theme attempt to introduce students to other cultures in the far reaches of the globe. One year, younger classes chose to produce a colourful collage of the world's flags. Another time, Australian and African animals were studied and drawn, then displayed in the hallway.

As part of the senior art program, students were introduced to a significant number of world cultures through the teaching of art history. Students chose a Renaissance artist, for example, researched his life and then attempted to model the artist's style in their own drawing or painting. In using art to learn about other countries, their wildlife and people, students gained a better understanding of where Inuit culture fits into the overall global picture. I found that my students were often astonished by the differences in the lives of people in other cultures. Upon reflection, however, they were mostly content to be where they were and very proud to be Inuit.

Often, during times of fiscal restraint, the first program cuts occur in arts education. Researchers agree that arts programs offer opportunities for children and youth at-risk to learn new skills, expand their horizons and develop self-esteem and well-being.

Arts programs provide crucial building blocks for healthy development in places of safety and through interaction with caring adults. Perhaps most importantly, involvement in the arts helps students develop a sense of community and place. Arts education is an effective means of integrating the traditional subject areas and makes schooling relevant for those students who need to see a more direct line between their school learning and their own lives.

Inuit art is recognized worldwide and has experienced a huge surge in popularity over the past seventy or more years. Many historians attribute the beginning of modern Inuit art to James Houston's arrival in the Arctic in 1948. Houston's trip north marked the beginning of a new, contemporary period in Inuit art. Carvings, prints, tapestries, paintings, and many other crafts and artwork have been made available to the world since the Houstons lived in Cape Dorset on Baffin Island.

Today, traditional skills are being turned into economic opportunities all across Nunavut and the Northwest Territories, which strengthens individual communities and allows the world at large a glimpse of life in the Arctic. During my time in the Baffin, almost every northern community offered local artwork to be purchased at the Co-op or Northern Store. Visitors to these communities buy up a large proportion of the art but Inuit themselves are buying it as gifts for friends and family and to adorn their own homes. In larger centres, Inuit art can be bought in art galleries, museums and craft shops. Soapstone carvings are probably the most renowned of Inuit art, but northern arts and crafts come in a host of other materials – antler, bone, ivory, animal hides, and others. Even traditional Inuit clothing, made of seal, caribou, polar bear and muskox skins, designed for the Arctic climate, has been transformed into unique Canadian fashions. Visitors to Iqaluit, Nunavut's capital, can purchase sealskin vests, muskox wool hats, caribou mittens, and many more creatively fashioned pieces of clothing.

Many Inuit today earn part of their living through the sale of their carvings, prints, drawings, paintings, and fabric arts (skin clothing and wall tapestries), as well as jewelry and tools. There are more artists per capita in the North than anywhere else in Canada. A significant portion of the economy in the Arctic relies on the sale of Inuit art. It is not unreasonable to assume that, given the appropriate guidance and opportunity, many Inuit students will also be able to make a living through their art. Teaching students how to present their work in a marketable fashion as well as how to price and sell their work are valuable skills to be taught in a senior art program in Nunavut. Perhaps more than many other places in the country, the pursuit of art as a career may offer many Inuit students a happy and rewarding lifestyle consistent with their cultural identity.

The senior class was enthusiastic at the prospect of organizing the first Umimmak School Art Show and Sale. They had worked non-stop for a week or so choosing art from their portfolios gathered over the year. They had also made specific pieces just for the show and sale. The students presented a vast array of work for their friends and family to view. Of course, foremost in their minds was the thought of how much money they could make if they sold everything they thought they could. Pricing the pieces turned out to be the most difficult part of the preparation for the event. Some ventured over to the Co-op to study the prices of the arts and crafts on sale there. They really had to ask each other and their teachers how much they should expect for the artwork. This in itself was a learning opportunity they had not anticipated. Most underpriced their work as they did not feel that theirs was "art like in the store."

After considerable agonizing and weighing of the consequences of their chosen price (*Is it too cheap? Is it too much?*), the tags were stuck on the items and placed on the tables. Drawings and paintings had been matted with colourful Bristol board and hung on the walls of the classroom and nearby hallway. Jewelry, made mostly from Fimo polymer clay, was beautifully displayed in handmade origami gift boxes on strategically placed fabric on tables. Their terracotta air-dried sculptured clay heads were placed on the same tables, mixed in alongside the boxes of earrings, necklaces, and brooches. Polar bears, seals, and snowmobiles carved into blocks of white plaster of Paris sat on tables waiting to be admired and, hopefully, purchased. Duffel socks and mittens, sealskin toys, *kamiks,* and crocheted hats added to the diverse works of art presented to the community by the students.

The high school class had graciously allowed the younger students to display their artwork for sale as well. Coloured doilies, glitter-glued pages of people and animal pictures rested next to the tissue-paper "stained-glass" windows and crayoned kaleidoscopes made up of student names. Lootie, the artist who had come into the senior classroom earlier in the year to teach carving techniques, had brought some of his own work in for sale as well. He displayed his carving and jewelry portfolio on the table beside his pieces. Needless to say, the Umimmak School Art Show and Sale presented a wide range of local artwork.

When the show opened, hordes of people rushed into the school and made their way to the senior classroom. It seemed that every parent in town had come to buy their own children's work. There was no squabbling about the prices – money was handed over without question. People moved about from table to table snatching up carvings, jewelry, and glitter art. Drawings and paintings disappeared from the walls. Students beamed as they listened to the compliments from all of the community art critics in the room. They had forgotten about their preoccupation with the money they would earn as a result of the show. They were being richly paid in praise and acknowledgement from their families and friends.

In that one single event, students learned more about art, and the potential of being able to earn at least some part of their living through art, than any teacher could have taught them from the front of a classroom. They learned how to work co-operatively with others in the planning of an important event; they learned about leadership and responsibility; they had to prioritize which work they would include in the exhibit and determine what price to ask for it; they learned how to finish and present artwork for a show and how to display their wares in a pleasing way to attract buyers. Crucially, students experienced first-hand the positive reactions of people to their creations, boosting their self-esteem and confidence by leaps and bounds. Not one student went home that evening without an enhanced pride in their ability and a feeling of strong cultural identity in being an Inuit artist.

9

It Takes a Village

Being a small school in a small community, it could easily be assumed that everyone would immediately know about what was happening at the school and vice versa. This is not the case. Despite over a third of the community population spending each day in the school, great efforts had to be made to ensure meaningful and respectful communication between the school and the inhabitants of the village. It is easy to become wrapped up in the day-to-day routines of the classroom and school, and to not share enough of the events of the day with parents and the community at large.

An added obstacle in the North stems from the fact that schools are still seen to be southern-based institutions, with little connection to the everyday Inuit life experience. Even in the south, parents are often intimidated at the thought of entering their child's school. This fear is magnified in the North. Very few northern schools boast a majority Indigenous staff – most teachers are non-Indigenous, English-speaking, and come from southern locales. Language is problematic in a school where many unilingual English-speaking teachers deal with the children of unilingual

Inuktitut-speaking parents. As a result, schools are foreign to most parents and community members. Many community members have negative views concerning schools – most Canadians are now aware of the shameful history of residential schools for Indigenous people across the country. This issue compounds the hesitancy and general distrust of southern-styled educational institutions. The onus is on northern schools to take the lead and reach out to parents in whatever ways they can to help develop an inclusive and supportive school-community relationship.

The establishment and maintenance of culture-based schooling is very much dependent upon a strong sense of community ownership. In the early 1990s, the territorial government recognized that when parents feel the school belongs to them, they are more comfortable playing an active role in their children's schooling by providing direction and contributing to the implementation of that direction. That is, parents become real partners in the education process and view that role both as a right and a responsibility.

I found the strength of the school-community relationship in Grise Fiord depended a great deal on effective communication between teachers, members of the local education authority, parents and students, as well as with local government agencies and businesses. Although effective communication in itself is difficult to achieve, it is not enough to simply communicate well – a reciprocal relationship of mutual appreciation and understanding needs to be established so the relationship benefits both sides. In Grise Fiord, many strategies were implemented to develop these types of partnerships between the community and Umimmak School.

Educators throughout North America continually struggle to increase parental involvement in the everyday activities of their children's schooling. Teachers recognize that when parents support their children's learning, student achievement improves significantly. Children benefit from seeing their mothers and fathers interacting with their teachers in school. As in most places to the south, many parents in the North work or have home responsibilities and have little extra time to participate in school events, let alone time to give to schools as volunteers. If schools communicate with parents as often as possible, more may want to become involved in the school program in one way or another.

Most Umimmak School information was shared by written and spoken word, as well as through invitations to myriad types of school events. Letters and notes were sent home with the eldest children on a regular basis. Correspondence was always offered in both Inuktitut and English. A monthly newsletter, produced by mostly staff and students, went to each home and business in town. The articles were written in either language, then translated. As part of their Inuktitut language classes, senior students were involved in the translating along with the bilingual school staff. Newly acquired digital cameras allowed for colourful images to be inserted and a wide selection of computer software and technology resources helped to make the newsletter quite impressive.

There was never any lack of news to share. All students were involved in contributing articles. The primary students wrote in Inuktitut, by hand, so their parents could observe their progress in learning the Inuktitut syllabics. Each December these very young students would write letters to Santa Claus, exclaiming how good they had been and what they wanted for Christmas. Parents loved seeing their children's handwriting. The newsletter boasted artistic images from all grades, usually related to the particular themes the classes were involved with. Sometimes the newsletter carried articles related mostly to that school theme; other times it was a potpourri of topics. Senior students interviewed Elders or local business people or each other. Often, they were asked to express opinions on some issue of local importance. And of course, there were always lots of requests for help with a variety of school activities – a lunch, storytelling, the breakfast program, an upcoming assembly, and so on. After a parent volunteer baked a delicious apple crumble as part of the snack program, students raved about it so much at home that parents asked for the recipe to be printed in the next newsletter.

The school newsletter became a community newspaper of sorts. It was hoped that parents would eventually contribute articles to the publication. For some months, the newsletter was a joint venture between the school and the community Adult Education Program, run by Nunavut Arctic College. After YoAnne's first year teaching at the school, she took on an additional half-time position with the College as the community adult educator. It became easy to blend some activities between the college students with those at Umimmak School. Writing for the newsletter allowed the community adult learners to improve their literacy and gain experience with writing in both languages. Their articles were published alongside those of the school. On some occasions when the school photocopier was not working properly, local businesses made the copies for us as a community service. The newsletter soon became a school communiqué that many parents and community members looked forward to receiving each month. We knew we were doing something right each time we were asked when the next edition would "hit the stands."

Community members also loved hearing the weekly school announcements on the local "FM," as the radio was referred to by people in town. Each Friday, an Inuit staff member, usually Mary or Mimi, collected informative class news from teachers and talked about those events in a thirty-minute segment during the morning broadcast. If there had been a school assembly, for example, all students receiving award certificates would be announced on the radio. Particular students would be congratulated for their achievements. Reports on recent activities as well as notices of upcoming events would be given. Students too were encouraged to speak on the radio. Mimi and Mary would often phone the station during school hours and have students take turns giving their own announcements. Sometimes an entire class would walk over to the Hamlet building and squeeze into the cramped quarters of the radio station to present their messages over the airwaves.

The radio was used throughout the year as a way to reach parents as they sat in the comfort of their own homes. The residents of Grise Fiord loved the "call-in" format of a radio show. Whenever the school needed to hear the opinions of the community concerning any issue, a summary of that issue would be delivered over the FM, either by an education council member or the principal, followed by residents calling in to the station to express their thoughts and ideas. Everyone in town would have the radio turned on, even in the businesses and offices. School goals, school year calendar dates, spring camp locations, school improvement plans, and the like were all issues that were discussed in part over the radio. Many people called in to offer opinions, no matter the topic. In using this valuable local resource, we were able to quickly gain an understanding of what the community expected on several important school topics.

To further develop meaningful partnerships with parents, and to enhance the lines of communication, activities were planned to encourage people to spend time together. As described earlier, the September picnic and scavenger hunt brought many people together at the beginning of the school year. Not long after the start of classes, teachers were encouraged to make "home visits" to the parents of their students. For a teacher new to the community, this always meant walking from house to house with someone who could interpret the conversations. In a community as small as Grise Fiord, home visits can be completed in one or two afternoons. Not only do these visits allow teachers and parents to meet face to face early in the school year, they ensure that the first official teacher meeting takes place in a non-confrontational manner away from the school. It is the teacher who is the visitor to the parents' home, not the parent visiting the school.

I always made a point to brief new teachers so they knew what to expect during those first visits. Teachers learn so much more about a student, his family, and cultural background through spending time with their family in their home. Even a quick visit early in the year is helpful. Sometimes teachers only stayed for fifteen minutes or so, sometimes long enough to share a pot of tea. Often, little conversation occurred. The point was to let community members know that teachers were open, willing, and ready to discuss students' progress with their parents anytime, anywhere. Teachers made regular visits to student homes throughout the year, and many of those visits became more social than official as people got to know one another.

Parents were invited to school events throughout the year. Sometimes an individual teacher would simply send invitations home with their students so that parents could attend an "end-of-theme" party in the classroom. Parents could view their children's class work and celebrate the learning that had occurred over the previous month or so. There was always cake and juice served during these "parties," followed by the playing of games.

Special spaghetti and lasagna dinners were held periodically to encourage even more community members to venture into the school. In the space of two hours after school, usually on a Friday, the hallway would be turned into a café, complete with checkered tablecloths, candlelight, and music. Ground caribou or muskox meat was the preferred ingredient in the meat sauce and when it was featured on the menu, it was "first come, first served." Most families in town showed up for the dinner events.

One year, a new teacher, Stephen, arranged to have the McDonald's store, in Yellowknife, fly out frozen Big Macs and Quarter Pounders as part of a fundraising campaign for a school trip. People in town had only seen McDonald's commercials on television. Some may have visited a restaurant in their travels, but most had never before eaten a McDonald's hamburger. Needless to say, the event was a huge success with the community. However, it was not repeated due to the enormous cost of airlifting food all the way from Yellowknife.

Any event that included food was an automatic success. The sharing of food, gathering around a meal, and feasting are all cultural traditions that are still greatly celebrated and enjoyed. Potluck lunches were held in the school hallway on numerous occasions. At one time, a sixteen- by twenty-four-foot canvas tent was erected in front of the school for an outdoor potluck that everyone in town attended.

Big event "open houses" were organized where students and teachers would develop displays and activities for parents to participate in. Stations were set up in classrooms, manned by students. Performances were staged in the hallways. One particular open house in early November stands out in my memory. The students had prepared their displays weeks in advance. Classrooms and hallways were jam-packed with posters and evidence of their hard work. The activity stations were prepared on the afternoon of the big event. Each student had a specific project they wanted to work on during the evening's open house. The primary class had been practising songs, and the elementary class had been busily producing arts and crafts projects all week. The junior and senior high classes focused on math, science, and computer activities.

The turnout was tremendous. I could do nothing but gaze in wonder over the sea of heads surrounding me in the hallway at the entrance to my classroom. Every classroom was packed with people of all ages. Toddlers, Elders, babies in mothers' *amautis*, fathers, and businessmen all crowded around the students at their projects. The dissection trays of earthworms, fetal pigs, and frogs in the senior classroom were very popular. Some students led parents in the process of dissecting a fresh specimen. Others demonstrated how to view the specimen under a dissecting microscope. A group of students had set themselves up in another corner of the room with drawing boards and easels, painting with watercolours and drawing each other. Many parents did some drawing of their own. Parents had to wait in line for many of the activities.

Computers were relatively new to the school and the novelty of sitting at a colour terminal to play word or mathematics games proved irresistible. The junior high class had taken on the computers as their main project that night. Each of them sat at a terminal, with two or three adults by their side, as they navigated their way through the games. Everywhere I looked I could see students and adults engaged in teaching and learning with each other. Optical illusions and math puzzles occupied another group, while some parents were making their own crafts in the elementary classroom down the hall.

At one time, excited voices of very young children could be heard near the main entrance – they were gathering people to listen to their songs. Within minutes just about everyone was squeezed into the primary classroom to watch the show. Proud parents smiled from ear to ear as their children sang in Inuktitut followed by English, and then Inuktitut again. Cameras flashed and videotape rolled.

The evening lasted for nearly three hours and by the end everyone was exhausted, but the celebration was well worth the effort. Students were proud of themselves and teachers were happy to have seen so many parents in the school. In that one event, the school had become a much less intimidating place for parents and community members.

Like the open houses, the science and math fairs attracted many parents, as did the yearly science and technology competitions in the gym. Each year parent judges were recruited for the competitive events and the entire community was invited to view the displays and then the awarding of the certificates and prizes.

Events like these are crucial in the development of partnerships between the school and the people of the community. For parents to feel they have ownership of the school, they must be involved in the decisions, big and small, that are made at the school that impact the lives of their children. It is the parents who must help create the vision of the school program for their children and they need to remain diligent in ensuring that the school continually reflects that vision.

"Community Visioning" meetings and workshops had taken place in most Baffin communities in the early to mid 1990s. School staff, education council members, parents, community members, students, and Elders gathered over several meetings to determine what each school should be teaching and what would be the characteristics of a school that could promote that knowledge. The results eventually became the basis for the strategies suggested in the Baffin Divisional Board of Education document, *Our Future is Now . . . Implementing Inuuqatigiit.*

As YoAnne and I arrived in Grise Fiord in the fall of 1995, "Visioning" was still in its infancy within the community. Harry, the principal, had engaged the Education Council and community in introductory meetings, where a preliminary direction was determined for Umimmak School. That fall, a more detailed plan was developed outlining where the community wished to see the school in the next year, then five years, and then the next ten years.

When I took over as principal in 1996, one of the first steps towards realizing this direction was to develop school goals that reflected the wishes of the community as well as the developing philosophy of the Baffin Divisional Board of Education. The "Visioning" information gathered the year before was reviewed early in the first term with staff, education council members, and with the community via the radio and notices distributed in town. A great deal of community input was used in the development of those school goals. I believe that in going through this process, parents and community members became real partners with the school and contributed in important ways to the education of their children at Umimmak School.

10

Community Partnerships

In a small isolated community, it is impossible to treat parents and community members separate from local business people and government workers. With so few people in town, everyone knows everyone else's business, and the lines between home and work become blurred. Fortunately, in Grise Fiord, this fact operated in our favour. There were several partnerships that developed between the school and specific community groups that added to and benefited the school program.

Across North America, a wide variety of educational studies link after-school program participation with improved attitudes toward school, higher expectations of school achievement, better work habits, and higher attendance rates. In Inuit communities like Grise Fiord, due to a lack of many formal types of youth organizations, after-school programs take the form of any variety of community activities, ones that are often related to a cultural tradition. Sometimes, due to the tremendous learning potential of these events, time is taken from the scheduled school day as well as time outside of school hours. A student in the Maritimes, for example, may head to a Boys and Girls Club after school, whereas students in Grise Fiord may go out on the land with a hunter from the community. They may go to the shore to unload sealift supplies for the Hamlet, or help build furniture for the local daycare facility. In Arctic communities, the boundary between school and after-school programs is fuzzier than in southern towns. I have, however, seen northern students derive the same benefits from participation in these activities as their southern counterparts.

Collaboration between school and community-based organizations can help students develop lasting academic and life skills. Researchers have found that students who participate in community organizations expressed a sense of personal value and empowerment far greater than did their peers who did not participate in some community-based organization. Simply put, students felt valued by adults. This regard boosted their self-confidence and changed their attitudes toward personal responsibility. Students' lives inside and outside of school become interwoven, and what students experience outside of school is crucial to their success in school. Adults inside and outside of school can use their resources together to strengthen learning in ways that go beyond what they could accomplish alone.

Several difficulties arise for students who encounter a school culture at odds with their home and community culture. Although a minority within the community at large, English-speaking, non-Inuit teachers are the dominant culture in the school. Community involvement in the school helps to empower students – it links the beliefs, values, and attitudes of their cultural community with those of the school culture. While living and teaching in the Baffin region, I observed that attention to the Inuktitut language and Inuit cultural activities within the school program and in after-school activities helped to enhance these connections.

Most northern schools have developed a local "resource bank" – a list of people and businesses that could benefit the school program in any number of ways. These lists are often made but people and groups are rarely called upon to contribute to the school in any meaningful way. In Grise Fiord, we strived to make sure that healthy partnerships were developed with community groups as well as with individuals. Sometimes seemingly small efforts paid off tenfold.

As a gesture of community spirit, junior and senior high students went out in pairs into the community each month with computer "cleaning kits" to perform basic mouse and keyboard maintenance on all of the computers in town. This meant visiting the Hamlet and Housing offices, the Health Centre, the Co-op, the Hunters and Trappers Organization, Renewable Resources, and Arctic College. Students enjoyed practising and showing off their skills, and community employers received a useful service in return. Any individual with a computer at home also received that same service. As their computer skills improved, some of the senior students were then invited to help businesses troubleshoot problems that arose. Andrew became quite adept at fixing frozen screens. Other students helped set up hard drives, printers, and modems. When students were able to successfully solve a computer problem for someone at the Hamlet or over at the Resource office, their pride was evident in the wide grins on their faces when they returned to the school. After experimenting with new drawing software, senior students designed computer-generated town maps with legends in three languages. They placed these maps throughout town for the benefit of tourists to the community.

One of the most rewarding partnerships the school developed was with Nunavut Arctic College. In the first two years that YoAnne and I were in Grise Fiord, there was no adult education facility, only a small office in the trailer next to the Health Centre. With permission, the school was used in the evenings and on weekends for college courses. Teachers at the school began offering their services to teach evening courses for the College. Harry, and then Stephen, taught English upgrading. YoAnne became the instructor for all of the computer courses. After the interest shown by parents at an open house at the school, I taught drawing and painting to adults in the evenings as well. The College bought as many of the supplies as they could for these courses, and when needed, the school chipped in with other supplies. In exchange for the use of the school facility and for the borrowed odds and ends, the College contributed an extra computer, a photocopier, paper, pens, ink cartridges, math compasses, and a collection of art supplies to the school.

More and more community people began asking for additional college courses. In the long dark season of the High Arctic, evening and weekend courses are very popular. Courses in Grise Fiord were well attended, more so than those offered in some of the larger surrounding communities. Creativity was the key. To encourage literacy amongst the adults of the community, an adult educator began teaching parents how to encourage reading with their children, and involved the students and preschoolers in the program. This "reading circle" took place each Sunday in the school (since that was where all of the books were), offering parents an opportunity to read to their children as well as spend quality time with them.

By this time, YoAnne was the Adult Educator for the community. Both the school and the college worked together to develop programs or specific community events. A sharing of resources seemed to be the natural direction in which to move. The main goal from a community perspective was to encourage lifelong learning and to get rid of the artificial barriers between the K-12 school and the College. The College eventually rented a vacant house in town as its Community Learning Centre, and although the school was no longer required for classroom space, the close partnership that had developed continued to grow.

Umimmak School became increasingly well equipped with computer technology resources, used by K-12 students during the day and adult learners in the evenings. Some teachers at the school still worked as instructors for some of the evening and weekend adult education courses. The College began to hire outside instructors to deliver specialty courses for people in town. Many were interested in the community administration program courses, as well as the outfitters and guide program. Although not generally Nunavut Arctic College policy, four senior students were able to participate in that first Guide Training course offered in the community. A well-respected Inuk from Pangnirtung travelled to

Grise to instruct the course. As it turned out, YoAnne and I knew Joavie from our years teaching in Pang. The following year, one of the school's students travelled to another community for three weeks to receive the next level of training. Working together with the College enabled the school to present students with many more opportunities like these. Similarly, college students were able to access school resources and staff as well.

The Community Health Representative, who worked out of the local Health Centre, offered her time to the school each Wednesday or Thursday to work mainly with the junior high students. Meeka had three children, two of whom were in school at the time. She and YoAnne would plan together and present high interest health-related topics to the adolescents of Grise Fiord. Topics included sex education, alcohol and drug abuse issues, and a variety of others. Students enjoyed Meeka's visits. She spoke with them in Inuktitut as much as possible and brought with her posters and pamphlets. Meeka also offered a pre-natal nutrition course to the senior high students. At that time, four students were already parents, another one was pregnant, and most of them were sexually active. Supplies for the courses were paid for by the Health Centre, and the kitchen facility, for the cooking of the nutritional foods, was provided by the school. This partnership not only benefited the school, it also allowed the Health Board to work towards its mandated role of community health education.

The Nurse-in-Charge visited the school at least once a week, not always for a medical visit, often just to visit with students at recess time. Cathy had arrived three months prior to YoAnne and me. She had worked in other Baffin communities and with Inuu in Labrador. With her calm, relaxed manner, she was able to build trusting relationships with all of her patients. Cathy listened well and students liked her. When possible, she preferred seeing the students in the school. Sometimes it was less intimidating for them in the school than at the clinic, depending on what it was she needed to do. Any eye tests or hearing tests and almost all of the vaccinations of the children were done at the school. Cathy would choose the bravest students first so they would not be crying as they returned to their classrooms from the makeshift clinic near the office. She usually had lollipops or some sort of treats hidden somewhere in her bag for the youngest children.

The senior students showed great interest in Cathy's talks about sexually transmitted diseases and contraception. We had been learning about STDs in our Human and Personal Development course. Having the community nurse confirm the existence of STDs in town made the learning all that more meaningful to the students. Needless to say, the condoms, pills, IUDs, and various contraceptive devices that Cathy brought with her were also of high interest. She allowed small groups to tour the Health Centre to learn about the science that went on in the clinic each day. Older students were allowed to use the autoclave for their microbiology experiments. After PJ broke his ankle, Cathy (and PJ of course) gave permission for a junior high camera crew to videotape the application of a plaster cast to his leg and the subsequent removal of that cast several weeks later. PJ's classmates were able to view the entire procedure from start to finish. Imagine the learning that could occur if all lessons were as authentic, hands-on, and meaningful as this.

Any time a health care specialist visited the community, they were asked to talk to the senior students about careers in the health care field. There is such a need for Inuit in all of the professions (especially health care and education) that it seemed silly not to take advantage of these visitors and give students a glimpse into possible career options. Visits by real doctors, mental health workers, counsellors, occupational and physiotherapists, and audiologists all contributed to the Career and Program Planning credit requirement for the high school students.

For years, the Co-op's board of directors attempted to keep the costs of fresh fruit and produce as reasonable as possible at its retail store. This allowed families to eat healthy foods without going broke. The cost of transporting food by air is extremely high all across the Arctic. Most visitors to Grise, however, were quite surprised by the cost of many food items – they were often lower than in larger Baffin communities, including Iqaluit. It is no secret that children learn better when they eat healthy foods; to that end, the Co-op donated two cases of apples, each and every week, to the school for an afternoon snack at recess time. And the school received a 10 percent discount on any food purchases. In return, the school purchased supplies locally whenever possible, always giving the store the opportunity to match prices with out-of-town suppliers. The monthly school newsletter acknowledged any help from the Co-op so the community was always aware of its support for the school.

Since the Co-op was the only store in town, it was important for the community to view the store as having an active role in community life, not just in the selling of goods for profit. Prizes were often donated by the store for special school and community events. When there were general attendance problems one winter and students were often later for class after lunch, the management and staff of the Co-op helped to enforce a "no-students-in-the-store" rule during regular school hours. Although not popular with some students, this helped the school a great deal.

A partnership with the Hamlet of Grise Fiord also proved beneficial. The school was the designated community emergency shelter. One early winter blizzard had practically the entire community population spending the night sleeping in every inch of the school. Sleeping bags were everywhere – it was a gigantic pyjama party! Adults and children roamed the classrooms and halls all night long. The school had been used as a safe place on numerous occasions during severe weather, but not all instances resulted in overnight stays.

The Hamlet offered many services to students at the school. When we needed a place for the senior boys to make their own harpoon heads, the Hamlet allowed a local artisan to use their garage for the project. There were many times when the school had need of propane torches and other specialized tools and the Hamlet often helped. When the school budget could no longer be stretched to purchase Christmas presents for every child in town, the Hamlet became involved and took care of the entire expense. For several years, the school and the Hamlet jointly applied for funding to develop a nutritious snack program at the school. We were able to offer snacks to students at every morning recess for all the years that I taught in Grise.

Whenever possible, students were encouraged to develop a civic responsibility. One particular spring, there was a serious water shortage. The water storage tanks were almost dry and the entire town went on rations. Senior male students were excused from school for nearly three weeks so they could help chip nearby icebergs and deliver the fresh ice to the town's water silos. We barely made it through that crisis, but with the students' help the Hamlet managed to maintain a minimal water supply until the glacier-fed river thawed and a new supply of fresh water was available. Although a potentially dangerous situation, this opportunity was an excellent way for students to learn about citizenship and active community involvement.

The Hamlet supported a policy that discouraged the hiring of any students who dropped out of school. This policy had been in place for a couple of years prior to my arrival. It was a way for the Hamlet to show that the education of community youth was valued and important. I must admit, however, that fewer people supported these actions as time went by. With the implementation of a senior high school program, young adults were now considered as students. Exceptions had to be made. If older students, with children of their own as well as household responsibilities, required extra income, they needed to be considered for work at the Hamlet on a part-time basis.

The fire department and the school worked together to provide very popular interactive drills with students. We were mandated to have six fire drills each year. Usually the fire department was warned that the alarm would sound at a predetermined time so they would know it was only a test run. One autumn morning the fire chief came into my office and suggested I set off the alarm at a specified time, but he would not notify his men of the drill in advance. He wanted to see how quickly the volunteers could mobilize and get to the school in full uniform with the firetruck ready for action.

As agreed, I pulled the alarm and began patrolling the hall to make sure teachers and students exited the school as quickly and safely as possible. As I turned the hall corner, Jeffrey, one of my senior students, nearly ran me down. Unbeknownst to me, he was a volunteer firefighter. He flew out the front door as hordes of students began to leave their classrooms. The large speaker on the roof of the school blared out the siren sound. Less than six minutes later, everyone was standing at a safe distance from the school as the fire truck rolled up to the front doors with all of the uniformed men in tow. By then the firefighters knew this was a drill, but they continued with their duties. They rolled out the hoses and searched each classroom.

Students learned more from this drill than they would have simply responding to the usual in-school fire drill. Children watched their fathers, uncles, and friends acting in a serious, professional manner as they honed their skills in responding to the siren, dressed in their firefighting gear, mobilizing the fire truck, after having arrived quickly on the scene. We practised these active drills several times a year. Sometimes, pre-selected students were purposely left in the imagined "burning schoolhouse" so firefighters could practise searching for students who were unaccounted for by their teachers as they conducted their head counts outside. Students took great pleasure in timing the firefighters' arrival, but they also knew exactly what to do and what to expect if a real fire did break out.

There were one or two comical situations that arose, but only due to the fact that these were drills and not actual fires. One October, at the request of the chief again, we planned another surprise drill. Unfortunately, someone had unplugged the fire engine battery the previous night and the truck would not start. It was a sorry sight to see three firemen arrive at the school carrying buckets of water. No doubt the chief had some choice words to share with them that afternoon.

One year, when the Hunters and Trappers Organization received considerable funding close to the end of their fiscal year, they donated a generous portion of the money to the school for land-based activities. A huge double-walled canvas tent was purchased for the school and weekly land trips were provided by the HTO from February through May. During this time, all equipment, supplies (including gasoline) and personnel were provided to the school. Each year the HTO awarded two muskox tags to the school, which enabled students to learn how to harvest muskox with experienced hunters. The school organized the trip and provided at least one staff member for the activity. The *qamouti* (sleds) were always packed for an overnight stay in case of inclement weather. Participating students changed each year – most times a multi-aged group was chosen so that older and younger students could spend time with one another. The hides of any animals successfully hunted stayed with the school and the meat was shared with community members, usually at a feast shortly after.

The first time I went out on the muskox hunt was with a young junior high group of students. Tookilkee, a respected hunter, his son, and another young hunter were our guides. We left town on six snowmobiles pulling three covered *qamouti* with boxes full of hunting and camping supplies. Happy, excited students tightly squeezed onto the sleds. We travelled east around the point of land visible from the community – we were aiming for a location less than two or three hours from town, where a herd of muskox had been seen recently. It was several hours before we arrived at the desired spot as we stopped often to investigate a number of seal breathing holes. It was hoped our guides would catch a seal for a fresh meal that afternoon. That particular time, we were not lucky.

As we approached the shoreline again, Tookilkee sighted a herd of muskoxen far off in the distance, up on the plateau at the base of the mountains. Even though I had lived in the North for several years, I was still amazed at how an Inuk can see small details so many kilometres away. I did not see those beefy mammals until much later as we followed the guides up onto the boulder-strewn land and, driving our snowmobiles, we shepherded the herd into the distinctive defence position that muskoxen are known for. For many students, this was the first muskox hunt they had been on. Two animals were harvested that day. They were skinned and butchered on the sea ice below the plateau. Students used their knives to help in the preparing of the meat. A biology lesson ensued as stomach contents were studied to see what the animal had been feeding on, and the intestines, liver, lungs, and heart were examined. All parts of the animal were kept. Attention was paid to keep the head and horns in good shape so that the finished skin and fur would look as good as it possibly could.

As with most land-based activities, students were hungry to learn all that they could. Mosha was keen to take a lead in the cutting of skins and meat. Levi was ready for everything the guides asked of him. Neither of them was afraid of getting their hands dirty. Karlye knew exactly when to get the stove going for hot water. All of them knew when to help and when to stay out of the way. I was always genuinely impressed how many of the students who did not stand out academically in school became the natural leaders and "stars" on the land trips. It was during these activities that teachers learned the most about the students and their rich lives outside of school.

Most people assumed that when a police officer showed up at school it was because a student was in trouble for one reason or another. The turnover of police officers in Grise Fiord was high. Grise was a single officer detachment and in four years I worked with three different officers. Most police understand the value in building relationships with youth outside of law-related issues. Two of the three officers in Grise were quite visible in and around the school, often visiting just to "touch base" with the students. At Umimmak School, the RCMP offered gun and boat safety presentations each year. Students really enjoyed these special events.

A national program had begun several years prior to my arrival in Grise Fiord, where one day each November, grade 9 students went to work with their parents instead of going to school. Grise had already identified career planning and the acquiring of job skills as priorities for the youth of the community. The Take Our Kids to Work program allowed students to experience the types of jobs available in their community and to see what skills and qualifications were needed for those jobs. Employers got an extra worker, free of charge, for the day.

Instead of limiting the program to grade 9 students – there were too few – everyone in grades 6 through 12 participated. Students identified where and with whom they wanted to work. Community members were sent letters and then contacted in person to arrange the working partners for the day. Some students wrote personal notes to community employees, expressing an interest in working with them. Co-operating employers were asked to fill out evaluations afterwards, consisting of mostly open-ended questions for each participating student. The community threw themselves into this program. It was so successful and popular that these student workday sessions were arranged three or four times each year. In our last year at Umimmak School, employers were calling the school, asking for the dates of each upcoming session. Several senior students secured summer jobs as a direct result of participating in the Take Our Kids to Work program.

Some valuable partnerships were developed with agencies outside of the community. The partnering of the Nunavut Science Institute (Iqaluit) with Umimmak School presented some intriguing opportunities for students. A number of scientists had visited the school over the years to share information on research projects going on throughout Nunavut. Marine biologists and Coast Guard staff presented slides, videos, and the viewing of marine plankton to students as they described the North Waters project research underway at a large polynia (open sea water) east of Ellesmere Island. This interaction between students and working scientists had obvious benefits to students, and the scientists could satisfy the need of community input into their research, a mandated expectation written into most of their project proposals. For three years, a partnership with the Polar Continental Shelf Project enabled staff and students to visit the icecap on Devon Island to observe and participate in a climate change study. Community members were involved as well, all coordinated through the school.

One year, the Geological Survey of Canada had students and local people involved in a two-week prospecting course. Interest was high so the course was offered again the following year. One or two of my senior students earned their prospecting licence and were able to stake claims, if they ever wished. And finally, the University of Winnipeg requested student assistance in a snow contaminants project for two years. It was too expensive to send researchers all the way to Grise Fiord to collect snow samples so help was enlisted through the school. In return, a sum of money was donated to the school for educational supplies.

In *Our Future is Now, Implementing Inuuqatigiit*, the Baffin Divisional School Board described a vision for partnerships where schools were actively supported by and involved in their communities. It was expected that through more community involvement, schools would increasingly reflect the culture of the community in values, policies and procedures, environment, program, behavioural expectations, staffing, and leadership. As I witnessed in Grise Fiord, partnerships between the school and the community supported meaningful student learning with links to their everyday experience and community life.

11

What Did We Do Right?

From the outside looking in, life in a small, isolated community can appear quite simple and idyllic. On one level, perhaps it is. Beneath the surface, however, a surprising depth and complexity of connections exist amongst community members, parents, students, and school staff. Most would agree that the role and effects of the school are especially profound. The image of the school portrayed in this memoir developed over time – the school was and still is a work in progress. After receiving high school accreditation in 1995, Umimmak School continued to take shape and change over the years. Successfully integrating the K-9 program with the new secondary program took time, effort, and considerable experimentation.

Many factors affected the life of the school. Staff changes occurred from one year to the next, as did the local education council membership. Numerous programs were initiated – some were kept, some were dropped. Parental and community input into the school program evolved over time. The older students themselves matured from one year to the next – many made valuable contributions towards the future direction of the school. Although I was most certainly in a leadership role as the senior high teacher and then the principal of the school, I was but one member of a team of educators, para-educators, students, concerned community members, and parents. We all worked together, regardless of our position within the school.

What did we do to promote student success in school? Ensuring that a caring and positive, supportive environment existed within the school for each student and that relevant programs be offered to all students, as well as continually working towards the goal of involving the community with the school, all helped students to become successful in a variety of ways. Prior to the addition of the high school program in Grise Fiord, very few (if any) of the students would have advanced to a senior secondary education. After four years, two students graduated with a high school diploma. All but two of the original high school students succeeded in passing grade 10 and were able to continue on in grade 11 and 12. The integration of the secondary program with the existing K to 9 program helped to nurture social skills in all students of the school, as a result of the frequent use of cooperative and multi-aged groupings for learning.

We measured success holistically, taking all aspects of a student's life into account. Success was important in each of the academic, social, emotional, physical, and spiritual realms. I believe that focusing on Inuktitut language and Inuit culture in the everyday classroom, authentic community involvement with the school program, and ongoing staff development all contributed to the successes at Umimmak School. Throughout their time in school they acquired knowledge, skills, and attitudes to, hopefully, prepare them for their future lives in Nunavut and the world.

Language and Culture in the Classroom

Close attention was given to the wishes of the people of the community when it came to the education of their children. The "Community Visioning" meetings and workshops which took place in Baffin communities in the early to mid 1990s helped determine what each school should be teaching and outlined the characteristics of a school that could promote that knowledge. School staff, education council members, Elders, students, parents, and community members were all consulted with and involved in the process.

The results of those meetings became the basis of a long-term plan for the schooling of students in Baffin communities. *Inuuqatigiit* (meaning "Inuit to Inuit," in the sense of togetherness) articulates the knowledge, skills, and values which students need to learn from an Inuit perspective. The *Inuuqatigiit* document suggested that to ensure education is meaningful to all Inuit children, it should continue to be student-centred, process-oriented, culture-based, holistic, include Inuit history, and involve parents and Elders. A tremendous amount of effort was put into ensuring that Umimmak School embraced the *Inuuqatigiit* vision of education for Inuit children.

According to *Inuuqatigiit*, Inuit believe that children who are treated as individuals – with respect, acceptance, and enjoyment – will become strong and confident. This will lead to success in planning and problem-solving, an ability in communicating with others, independent thinking, and a desire to be strong in their own language. In order to achieve this in the present-day educational system, Inuit believe that school instruction must incorporate sensitivity to the Inuit perspective – learning should occur within a cultural context where possible, and use of Inuktitut language should also be encouraged. Even the way in which teachers and schools view the language of their students is an important contributor to student achievement.

Inuuqatigiit implies that subject lessons need to be related to Inuit history, knowledge, and experience as much as possible. A connection to the students' life experiences needs to be present in each lesson for the learning to be meaningful. Cultural differences in learning are especially apparent in learning styles, communication styles, and language differences. Cultural values and beliefs should not be excluded from the everyday learning of Inuit children. *Inuuqatigiit* tells us that it cannot.

Teachers who practise culturally relevant methods believe that all students can succeed. They see themselves as part of the community and teaching is a way of giving back to the community. Gloria Ladson-Billings, an American educational theorist, believes that teachers who practise culturally relevant methods have very specific traits. They have relationships that are fluid and equitable and extend beyond the classroom; they demonstrate a connectedness with all of their students and encourage the same between students; they encourage a community of learners; they encourage their students to learn collaboratively; they believe that knowledge is continuously re-created, recycled, and shared by teachers and students alike; rather than expecting students to demonstrate prior knowledge and skills, they help students develop that knowledge by building bridges and scaffolding for learning.

Within the Inuit context, an "*Inuuqatigiit* classroom" should encompass and reflect Inuit values, beliefs, and manners about learning; it has a discipline that is calm and quietly explained; there is meaningful use of Inuktitut language; class resources include many Inuit materials; activity centres include traditional items, as well as books and tapes in Inuktitut; there should be easy access to traditional tools, shelters, and equipment; many people from the community should be encouraged to visit the classroom on a regular basis. According to *Inuuqatigiit*, when these guidelines are followed there are many benefits: instruction will be more meaningful for students and attendance will improve; learning will be more fun for both student and teacher; student motivation will be higher; learning and sharing will be the student's main goal; the school will become more community oriented and parents will feel they have a say in the education of their child; there will be more sharing and understanding between the school and the community; students will show respect for elders and others; students will show pride in their language and culture.

Inuit elders and parents want to see a culturally relevant school system in place in Nunavut for their children. Communities want the youth of today to draw on the knowledge and wisdom of the past to take them into the next century. *Inuuqatigiit* suggests that traditional skills and wisdom combined with present-day knowledge and modern technology will enable Inuit youth to learn what is needed to succeed in their rapidly changing world and beyond.

Community Involvement

Not all learning occurs within the boundaries of the school. Youths spend many of their waking hours outside of school within their community. Growing evidence suggests that after-school program participation is associated with higher grades and test scores. In small, remote northern communities, highly structured and organized after-school programs seen in the south are almost non-existent. I will simply equate these types of programs with school-community activities.

Again, according to *Inuuqatigiit*, Elders believe that by including parents and community in identifying strategies that promote positive learning for Inuit children, healthy "helping" partnerships will be fostered within the community. Students will be empowered in the school context to the extent that their parents are empowered through their interactions with the school. I have no doubt that a large amount of student success at Umimmak School was a result of parental and community involvement in many aspects of the school program.

Staff Development

Teacher development may be the single most important key to improving schools over the long term. Schools should be learning and inquiring communities for both teachers and students. At Umimmak School, our small staff of five had to quickly learn to trust and depend on one another for the everyday demands of teaching in an isolated and challenging environment. In a sense, we had no choice but to work together towards making the school an enjoyable and effective place of learning. Our nearest sister school was hundreds of kilometres away and school board officials visited only once or twice a year. Basically, we were on our own for the day-to-day operation of the school.

Professional improvement workshops occurred throughout the school year, most often as in-school offerings. We relied on each other's expertise and willingness to share in order to cultivate our professional learning. Each week or so, staff would meet to plan for upcoming themes. Early school closures that had already been worked into the school calendar allowed these meetings to occur within school time so that teachers did not need to spend an inordinate amount of their personal time in the planning. Teaching teams of two would also determine their strategies together on a regular basis. Every couple of years a regional teachers' conference would take place, usually in Iqaluit, where all Baffin teachers would attend any number of workshops. Although most of these workshops, in my view, are quite informative and relevant to Northern teaching, it is the networking and informal meetings and get-togethers that teachers look forward to and truly benefit from. It is the one time when all Baffin teachers are able to share in their successes and frustrations, as well as share their personal school stories – it is a time where teachers feel connected to a larger community of professionals in much the same situations as themselves.

Of course, being able to get away for a few days is price-less when you work in a very isolated fly-in community. I recall a teacher conference in Yellowknife, in the early '90s, where it seemed that every female teacher in the Baffin had booked hair appointments either at lunch or late in the afternoon. Educators took advantage of exploring the capital city and patronized every restaurant and shop they could fit in during the off-hours! Teachers always returned to their home community feeling refreshed, invigorated, and ready to apply the new learnings throughout the rest of the school year.

In 1994, the Nunavut Boards of Education initiated a project related to the professional development of educators working in the school system. *Pauqatigiit* (meaning *paddling together*), involved the Federation of Nunavut Teachers, all community education councils, the Nunavut Teacher Education Program with its partner McGill University, and the Department of Education in collaborative efforts to meet the needs identified by Nunavut educators. This was a much welcome initiative to all teachers, Inuit and non-Inuit alike, working in isolated communities. Not only would it begin to address the multitude of educator needs in Inuit schools, it was also a homegrown initiative, developed in the North by and for northern educators.

I was lucky to meet several inspiring long-time Baffin educators early in my years in the North. Fiona O'Donoghue (now Walton) was a supervisor of schools at the Board office in the late 1980s. In her later research of professional learning in Nunavut schools she argued that ethically based professional practise requires that southern models be carefully scrutinized and evaluated as potentially violent intrusions and contributors to the exponential and endemic cultural and linguistic erosion that is part of a colonial legacy. She sees professional learning as one of the most powerful catalysts in the pursuit of freedom and the retrieval and maintenance of identity, language, and culture. O'Donoghue asserts that professional learning is key to addressing issues of difference, identity, and freedom within the school system. During the 1996-97 school year, 35 percent of Nunavut teachers in schools were Indigenous. If this number is to increase significantly, Inuit educators must feel empowered in their positions within the community as well as within the educational system. Sadly, even as recently as 2016, only 20 percent of teachers were Inuit.

Regardless of any "out of community" professional improvement initiatives or opportunities, the individual staffs of all community schools must work well together each and every day. Collegial relationships between staff that portray mutual respect and support of each other go a long way to enhance staff development. I have often referred to an idea of Roland S. Barth, a well-known American educator, when speaking of educational issues. He maintains that the quality of adult relationships within a school has more to do with the quality and character of the school, and with the accomplishment of students, than any other factor. This is a belief echoed by many. I believe that the teachers at Umimmak School modelled healthy and supportive collegial relationships for the student population. Ultimately, this may have added to the success of many students in the school.

12

Challenges to Success

While I believe that the overall program at Umimmak School was a successful one, it certainly did not always follow a smooth road. The story that has unfolded so far is not only my interpretation of the successes, it is also testimony to the many obstacles that present themselves along the path to student success in northern schools. Teaching anywhere is a monumental endeavour, but teaching in Nunavut presents some unique challenges.

Early in my northern teaching career, I was astonished to realize that the fifteen students that I saw on a Monday are not necessarily the same fifteen I see on a Tuesday. Attendance seemed to be an option. Unlike many school-aged children in the south, Inuit children appeared to possess great personal freedom. Many are allowed to stay out late with friends, often unsupervised, and are allowed to come and go as they please at all hours of the day and night. In small, close-knit communities this does not pose any danger to the children – everyone keeps an eye on them wherever they may be. They are safe. Children are not forced to get up in the mornings and go to school. If a child is tired or does not feel like attending school, he is rarely pushed to do so. Many cultural activities keep students away from school as well. Hunting and family camping, in spring and early fall in particular, account for a lot of absenteeism. As well, girls are often expected to babysit younger siblings while parents work or are busy elsewhere. Day-care facilities in the smaller Nunavut settlements are rare. As students get older the lure of working part-time and earning a paycheque seems to overtake the importance of attending school. Lateness and truancy are common problems in all Nunavut schools.

Although attendance statistics for Umimmak School had historically been fairly good, it was always a struggle to maintain that record. An ambitious main objective was to make school more interesting than any of the alternatives. We believed in the idea that offering a meaningful and relevant program to our students would in itself keep them coming to school each day. If we made parents aware of the importance of school for their children, then they would also work to keep them in school on a daily basis. As a staff, we constantly discussed attendance issues over the years and worked hard to improve attendance, especially with the older senior high school students. Getting them to come to school was something that we had to work at every single day.

Apathy is a difficult condition to overcome. Students find themselves in a psychological space where they are disinterested in everything presented to them. They may be bored, not adequately challenged, overly challenged, uncomfortable, wishing they were anywhere else ... there are so many reasons why a child becomes apathetic in school. No matter how fine a program may be, there will always be a number of individuals who have no enthusiasm at all. Sometimes this can spread throughout a class, from one person to another.

In comparing all of the schools I have taught in, Umimmak School suffered the least from apathy. However, one or two students in the junior high and senior high classes would show signs regularly after the initial novelty of the start of the year had worn off. Apathy often seemed to affect the adolescent students more. Staff continually strived to develop more meaningful lessons, where the learning was of interest to as many as possible. We had to find a hook, grab students' attention, and keep it for as long as we could. We tried to ignite their internal motivations. This is simply good educational practise. In a cross-cultural, second-language classroom situation, apathy may also arise due to any number of complex cultural reasons. Conversations between Inuit and non-Inuit staff, teachers, and community were crucial in developing strategies to keep students engaged in their daily school activities.

Discipline codes are as varying and different as are schools. Umimmak School is small enough that individual cases of inappropriate behaviour can be considered as they arise. This is not to say there was no code of conduct in school. Through constant modelling of appropriate ways in which to interact with others, through regular classroom discussions and through scheduled school assemblies, students learned that the only "rule" really necessary was to respect yourself, your classmates, teachers, and your family. If students at least attempted to honour this ideal, discipline was not a problem in school. Teachers and students would jointly decide on classroom rules and the consequences for breaking those rules at the beginning of each year.

All staff and students were responsible for reminding everyone of appropriate respectful behaviour. However, kids will be kids. We did have our share of heated arguments, temper tantrums, use of profane language, emotional outbursts, periodic playground altercations, and even a fist fight or two. The key here was to consider the individual student's circumstances, to remain as calm and quiet-toned as possible throughout the determining of what was to be done, and to be fair and consistent in applying the rules. I cannot say discipline was a big problem at Umimmak School, yet I realize this was probably a result of how individual cases were handled from the start and how everyone was diligent in maintaining that ideal of what we understood to be "a respectful school."

Each September, time was dedicated to students and community members meeting new school staff. Teacher turnover rates in the North generally are very high. In the four-year period of 1995 to 1999 at Umimmak School, YoAnne and I were the only non-Inuit staff who returned to the community each year. Harry, the principal before me, had remained in the community for two years, yet every other teacher stayed for only one year. There were diverse reasons for this short retention of staff in Grise Fiord.

These same factors come into play throughout most other Arctic communities as well. The simple issue of isolation from friends and family affected many southern teachers who came to Grise Fiord. Being one of the most northern communities in the world poses special transportation challenges. Few teachers could fly out at Christmas to be with family. Airline schedules, connections to other locations, and of course the unpredictable Arctic weather all combined to make travel quite difficult, never mind unreliable. Complete immersion within a culture and language different to their own proved too hard for some. The embracing of, or at the very least, the understanding of beliefs, values, attitudes, and perspectives of a land-based, Indigenous community was impossible for some. All of the things I admired and adored about Grise Fiord were difficulties to overcome for others.

With a population of 150, Grise seemed small and lacking in community resources for many. Some teachers could not come to grips with the effects of irregular attendance on their daily lessons; others disagreed with the community's perspective on the disciplining of children. Again, these were cultural perspectives that affected the life of the school to a large degree. Although the school was, in my opinion, very well equipped with teaching resources, some teachers tired of the constant struggle to develop their own meaningful, culturally relevant teaching materials. Teaching well in Grise Fiord could be overwhelming, both professionally and personally.

Simply put, teachers in the north are asked to do a lot – it is demanding work. Educators need to have a strong understanding of how to individualize instruction for a wide range of second-language students, who may have a history of spotty attendance, as well as an ability to individualize programs for integrated special needs students. Northern teachers require a good understanding of first- and second-language learning as well as an ability to accommodate students in an ESL situation. Any teacher in the

North needs to work effectively in a cross-cultural environment and have good programming skills in order to create relevant lessons for students. Teachers should have some first-hand experience, or at least an understanding, of isolation to better have a sense of the reality of living in a fly-in northern community.

I believe that personal attributes play a key role in determining if someone is suited to teaching in isolated Indigenous communities. From what I have seen, people who do best in small Arctic schools are those who are people-oriented, open-minded and flexible, accommodating, optimistic, self-confident, interested in the environment, and possess a love of the outdoors. An adventurous spirit is most certainly an advantage. People need to be comfortable in their own skin before they can tackle the challenges of living and working in a completely foreign environment. The strength of any personal relationship that they have with any number of people in the community – be they with other teachers or new friends in the community – can be the deciding factor in whether they flounder or flourish in their newly adopted home.

Teachers who come North with a partner or a friend seem to be able to more easily overcome many of the challenges. Having a trusted companion to talk to at the end of the day makes a world of difference. Couples can share in the new experiences, good and not-so-good. YoAnne and I moved to Pangnirtung together and then on to Hall Beach and Grise Fiord – the constant and reliable companionship only added to our collective experience throughout our time in the North. The strength of our personal relationship enabled us both to dig in and stay for a much longer time than we had initially planned. We loved working and living in the North and we still look back on that time as a wonderful adventure.

I am an optimist. I focus on the positive. I do admit, however, that I had to navigate my way through some tough periods while in the North. I felt frustration at times, with students, with colleagues, and with the community. I felt sadness then anger at what I perceived to be social injustices within the community. The smallness of everything got to me every now and then. When I became principal, I struggled with stress more than at any other time in my life. The weight of responsibility crushed me. I remember one night lying in bed feeling so overwhelmed that all I could do to release this emotion was to sob like a child until I fell asleep.

This was perhaps my lowest moment. It only happened once. YoAnne helped me through it and the anxiety passed. I had placed huge expectations on myself. I wanted to do everything well. Each year I would have to keep some space in my professional growth plan for working on ways in which I could more healthily balance my professional and personal life. I had to consciously make time for myself and not be at the school every evening and weekend. Many times I caught myself in my office at eight o'clock in the evening, still without supper. Most weekends I would be in school on a Saturday afternoon or Sunday morning. There really was no end to the amount of time you could put into the work as teacher. The fact was that even if you worked 24/7 there would always be more need than you could give.

I did learn to deal with the immense workload though. I became more efficient with time. To feed my emotional and spiritual self, I spent as much time outside as I possibly could. We always had a dog that needed walking. After Figgy Duff passed away, we brought Taqsaq, a purebred Dalmatian, to Grise Fiord. We bought a snowmobile and joined in with people on regular excursions, camping expeditions, dog team trips, and fishing trips. We participated in community events and visited people after school. We became involved in the life of the community. YoAnne and I hiked mountains and river valleys and cross-country skied up and down glaciers close to town. When I needed time alone, a quick zip out on the Ski-Doo to an ice-locked iceberg for sweet tea and a biscuit would work wonders. Distancing myself from town helped put everything into perspective. The Arctic land and ice are immense, the communities tiny, and the distances between them long. Breathing in the pure cool air in that wilderness, with the knowledge that there were no other villages for hundreds of kilometres in any direction, soothed my soul. This feeling always calmed me and filled me with a sense of awe.

There are enormous challenges for southerners teaching in northern communities. Promoting success in northern schools is a monumental task but it can be done. I have brought attention to just a few factors that may help make northern schools successful. I do believe that each small step forward strengthens the way in which the school is viewed within the community, and that the more community there is in the school, the better. My main understanding of all of this is that the lives of the students in the school, of the people in the community, and of the individual teachers who make up the staff are all interconnected and influence each other in very tangible and important ways. It is the group effort that makes a school successful.

13

How Did I End Up in the Arctic?

I feel privileged to have been able to live and work and interact with Inuit throughout the North. I have been involved in personal and professional activities that I would never have had the chance to experience anywhere else in the world. When I first arrived in the eastern Arctic, I brought with me a particular set of beliefs, values, and attitudes that were a function of my own culture and language, my own background in schooling, and my everyday experience. I soon realized that most of what I thought to be true about education in general, and about student learning, was not necessarily the only "truth." My outlook and overall philosophy, and how I taught, changed a great deal as I travelled from one Inuit community to the next.

Any person wishing to discover why they do the things they do, or why they hold the beliefs they do, inevitably finds themselves reminiscing about their past. We are all products of our past and present, of our family situation, of our particular culture and language. Our attitudes and beliefs are cultivated from the day we are born. In searching out reasons for my own feelings about education, I had to think back on my early childhood and school years.

Certain themes emerged, themes that were repeated again as I recalled later school memories and early work experiences. I began to identify what I call "defining moments" – moments in my life that became integral not only to my personal development but to my professional development as a teacher. Defining moments allow you to see connecting lines between pivotal times in your life that were previously hidden.

I believe that fate conspired to send me to the Arctic. Upon reflecting on my own life story and my personal development, it seems logical that I ended up teaching Inuit students in the High Arctic.

I was born in Scotland and spent my early years living in a number of small villages throughout Britain. I spent a lot of time outdoors playing in the woods or out on the hills. I remember climbing trees and cliffs and happily roaming about the countryside. Often, I would hide behind a large boulder, or a hedgerow, and sneak up on the sheep and cows in the pastures. I sometimes imagined myself a shepherd, tending to all of the animals, domestic and wild. I wandered everywhere and found myself temporarily lost more than once. A concerned policeman returned me to my parents on one particular occasion. I have a collage of memories of golden bracken fern, green fields, and mist and rain. I can still smell the mud of the riverbank, as I remember the white swans on the water. These early childhood themes of a love of nature and a desire to be outdoors followed me into my adult and professional life.

I received a traditional Western European schooling. I remember loving to read from an early age. I began school at age four in the south of England. Mum would walk me to school each morning with my brothers in tow in the pram. Perhaps, in the beginning, reading was fun because it came to me so easily. As a preteen I would read fairy tales (from a book I still own) to my two younger siblings – they would cuddle up in my bed and I would choose a story for the night. Later I remember losing myself in the adventures of storybook characters whom I came to regard as my friends. Those stories captivated me. I wanted to join Enid Blyton's

Secret Seven and *Famous Five* on all their adventures. My parents repeatedly caught me reading with a flashlight under the bedsheets at night.

My family immigrated to Canada when I was seven, where I entered an east-end Toronto school, filled with Italian and Greek children. This was my first experience with people of varying ethnic backgrounds. I remember being very curious about my classmates from such different cultures and families. Ten months later, my family moved again into the country on the southern shore of Georgian Bay and I entered yet another school (my fourth!). My parents put down roots this time – to this day they still live in Victoria Harbour, overlooking the waters of the bay.

I loved school and always did well academically. Although a few of my teachers along the way were not always the best educators, most were truly wonderful. I am sure that my desire to do well in school greatly affected my expectations as a teacher later in my life. My favourite teachers in high school taught art, math, and science. Madame Boucher was wild and creative, and encouraged artistic expression in all her students. A very strong-charactered, older woman was my senior math teacher – we all respected Mrs. Cardenas and appreciated how well she explained difficult concepts. Science intrigued me. One of the strongest "Aha" experiences I ever had in my life (a defining moment) was the result of science learning in tenth grade. Travelling home on the bus one day, I fixed my eyes on a huge boulder in the field and suddenly I realized I knew *how* it got there and *why* it was there. In my mind, I imagined the glaciers of ten thousand years ago dumping these rocky erratics all across the southern Ontario fields. I remember sitting on that bus with a silly grin on my face, confident in the fact that I understood something very profound.

Art has been a part of my life since the beginning. For as long as I can remember I have always been the "artist." I remember my Auntie Marion taking me to a frame shop at the ripe old age of four years so she could frame my coloured drawing of a First Nations Brave, sitting cross-legged in front of a teepee. I honestly have no idea where the inspiration for that drawing came from

– we were still living in Scotland at the time and I am sure I knew nothing about North America. Perhaps this was a glimpse into my future work with Indigenous people in Canada? Who knows? At any rate, I was always that kid in school who was known as the one who was good in art. It was simply part of me – I never had to work at it, I just happened to be someone who could draw. I loved sketching and painting especially.

However, I did not truly begin to appreciate my abilities until I entered high school. I became hypnotized by the incredible realism of the wildlife artists, and strived to be as good as Glen Loates, Robert Bateman, and James Fenwick Lansdowne. I remember practically forcing friends to sit at my kitchen table at home and admire each and every page of my new book, *The Art of Glen Loates*. I expected everyone else to be as enthralled with the art as I was. Of course, they were not, but they were polite. My senior biology teacher, Mr. Lovering, raved about my detailed colour illustrations of our rat dissections and I learned for the first time that I could go into the field of scientific illustration, if I wanted.

Even though I chose to study biology after high school, I always managed to find some illustration work along the way to satisfy my inner artist. I was lucky enough to work as a botanical illustrator for the University of Guelph for a full year after graduating from the wildlife biology program. As I worked as a naturalist I often secured off-season art contracts for indoor and outdoor park exhibits, posters, and various niche publications.

I feel fortunate to have had so many good teachers in my life. Surprisingly, most of them are memorable to me not because of their knowledge of any particular subject but due to the way they made me feel as a student in school. To be sure, this fact has propelled me, in my professional life as a teacher, to emphasize the development of interpersonal relationships with and among students in the classroom.

Throughout school, I tutored friends in need of help with various subjects. I did this because of my desire for others to enjoy and understand things the way I did. I liked helping people learn, and I discovered I was good at explaining concepts clearly. Many told me I should be a teacher, but the very idea of choosing a career that effectively confined me to the indoors was horrifying at the time. After all, I had plans for a much more glorious, outdoor life of adventure than could possibly be offered by a career in teaching.

On the day my parents dropped me off at the University of Guelph's student residence, I could not wipe the smile from my face. Freedom at last! I was a little nervous, but very excited at the possibility of determining my life's future direction. I enrolled in the Fisheries and Wildlife Biology program, and although it took a semester or so to find my groove, I thoroughly enjoyed university life. I socialized with a small group of wonderful people, mostly with whom I shared common interests. I eagerly soaked up the new information that was presented to me in the lecture halls and laboratories. Very early in my academic life, I became awe-inspired with Darwinian theory, evolutionary biology, and, of all things, invertebrate zoology. I discovered the essays of Stephen Jay Gould and the writings of Jacob Bronowski and Richard Dawkins. A whole new, intriguing world seemed to have opened up for me. In my future, I imagined myself a great Canadian naturalist.

In the spring of my second year at Guelph, the singularly most important defining moment of my professional life occurred. I secured summer employment with the Canadian Wildlife Service, working as a naturalist at the Wye Marsh Wildlife Interpretation Centre in Ontario. It was my seasonal work at this centre that would deepen my already profound respect and attachment for the natural world, and aid in the rediscovery of my desire to educate people in one way or another.

I returned to the marsh each summer throughout my university undergraduate years. I learned the names, both common and scientific, of practically everything that grew out of the ground. I studied the behaviour of wild animals to the nth degree. I arose at four o'clock in the morning for a full six weeks one summer to participate in a breeding bird survey. I discovered the joy of walking transects and identifying birds from their calls alone. A large part of my work at the marsh involved nature interpretation for the visiting public and school groups during May and June. I would lead nature walks and canoe excursions, give slide presentations, and provide demonstrations on a number of nature-related topics. Although most of the visitors to the marsh were interested in the outdoors already, I derived great pleasure in turning them on to the lesser-known mysteries of nature. Each autumn I would go back to the university with yet another full summer season of field experience to complement my studies in wildlife biology.

After graduation, I returned for one last summer at the marsh and then worked full-time for a year at the University of Guelph Arboretum. It seems that the director, Erik Jorgensen, had noticed my artistic ability while I was a part-time naturalist at the Arboretum's nature centre throughout the school year. Professor Jorgensen took me under his wing, creating a position just for me and hired me as a botanical illustrator. How important mentors are!

Technicians would bring me samples from the various plant collections of the university, and holding the twig or flower in my left hand, I would draw the fresh specimens with my right. A year later, after returning home from a six-month backpacking trip in Britain and Europe, I worked as an illustrator, designing outdoor wildlife exhibits for a provincial park. I then drove to Saskatchewan to work as a naturalist (where I also met YoAnne), followed with similar work in Newfoundland, Ontario, and New Brunswick. At some point between all of this contract work, YoAnne and I managed to fit in an extraordinary five-month safari in East Africa. For a long while it seemed my career was a perfect combination of nature illustration and interpretation.

After putting down roots in New Brunswick, YoAnne and I each decided to earn a teaching degree. Looking to the future, we felt we needed more secure work and a degree in education seemed to fit both of us. YoAnne attended the Université de Moncton while I enrolled at Mount Allison University.

Two specific memories stand out for me from that particular year in the Bachelor of Education program. The first one was a slap-in-the-face realization that not everyone was an environmentalist. There were actually people in this world who knew very little about the natural environment, and couldn't care less. I realized that after spending my entire life concerned with nature, I had subconsciously come to believe that everyone thought the same way when it came to environmental issues. I had managed to surround myself with like-minded individuals. Here, I met people training to become teachers who seemingly had no environmental conscience. This troubled me greatly.

The second defining moment of that year occurred as I observed a group of pre-service science teachers modelling a junior high science lesson. They were collecting insects from the "schoolyard" for later observation with microscopes in the classroom. Over a short period of time the insects were lured into a container of sugar water, drowning in the process. I instantly expressed my disappointment that teachers, through their actions, would encourage young students to senselessly kill living things, albeit insects, for such a frivolous cause. *Could the bugs not be trapped with a butterfly net and be observed as living creatures?* I was greeted with blank stares and was mildly teased about this for a while. But these actions seemed poor judgement to me. I believed that as science teachers we should encourage curiosity about the natural world but, more importantly, we should be instilling a value for all forms of life within our students as well.

In 1989, the week after I watched a documentary on the ecology of the Arctic by David Suzuki, entitled *The Nature of Things: The Edge of Ice*, an advertisement for teaching positions in the Baffin region of the Northwest Territories appeared in a national newspaper. The tagline, "Looking for an adventure?" was irresistible. We both applied and were offered jobs. In July of that year we moved to Pangnirtung, Baffin Island. The rest, as they say, is history.

14

Teacher as Student

After leaving Grise Fiord I entered a Master of Education program and spent considerable time reflecting on and analyzing my northern experience. I immersed myself in the writings of learning theorists, curriculum planners, and critical pedagogists. I shared a particular connection with Sylvia Ashton-Warner in reading her 1963 journal, *Teacher*, which documents her time educating Maori children in New Zealand. I began to write about my own experiences and thoughts about education. I took the time to step back and critically reflect on my own teaching practises. I reacquainted myself with my "inner voice." I began to articulate why I believe and do the things I do as a teacher and why I feel they are important.

I wondered to myself, *Am I ruined?* I wasn't sure whether any teaching job could compare to the fulfilling work I had been involved with in the Arctic. *Would it ever be possible to be truly excited to teach in a mainstream southern educational institution again?* I felt I had been involved in such a unique, challenging, and invigorating experience that it might not be reasonable to expect to feel that way about teaching again.

It Really Does Take a Community to Raise a Child

Living and working in the North has allowed me to truly understand the adage *It takes a community to raise a child.* I learned that community involvement is a key factor in the success of schools. I observed this philosophy in action. When all people concerned work towards the development of strong links between the school and its community, powerful things happen. Schools need to reflect the beliefs and values of their greater community. Working in the North has solidly convinced me of the importance of including the language and culture of the students in the school curriculum. I witnessed the value of students being able to regularly learn in their first language throughout their school years. And I understand that when students do begin learning in a second language, we need to be more patient and forgiving. Too many teachers focus on the less-than-perfect English skills of their second-language students. Should we not focus more on the fact that those same students are able to communicate in more than one language? We need to celebrate bilingual and multilingual students more often.

I admire the way Indigenous cultures revere their Elders. Respecting and valuing the wisdom of older members in society need to be taught and reinforced in schools in very real ways. I believe that Elders in any community should be integral to the school program at all levels. Imagine a school designed to include an Elders' meeting room where these wise members of the community can sit, have tea, socialize with one another, as well as actively participate in the school program by telling stories, demonstrating cultural skills or teaching language where needed. What an inviting school that would be!

Healthy Relationships

I have come to understand that school administrators play a key role in building a positive, healthy school culture. Attention to the quality of the personal interactions between the staff themselves, as well as with students and their parents, is of utmost importance. My main focus as a school principal became the developing of a respectful supportive environment in which teaching and learning could occur in a way that benefits all members of the school population. The perception that students have of how the adults in their school behave towards one another greatly influences the atmosphere of the school and eventual student success.

I learned that a school principal needs to model both a professional and moral style of leadership within the school as well as provide whatever support is needed to allow teachers to go about teaching. I appreciate the value of administrators who provide leadership in the ongoing, professional development of their staff. If teacher development is an important factor that leads to school improvement, then professional development for school staff should occur on a regular basis. The strengths of teachers on staff need to be both recognized and made use of in effective ways. As with students in the classroom, staff within the school need to feel appreciated and valued.

I see the importance of teachers being encouraged to develop a shared sense of purpose for their school. At Umimmak School, I attempted to make opportunities for shared decision making and problem solving available as often as possible. This helped to develop a collaborative approach – a style of shared leadership – within the school.

Schools are not just places of learning. Schools house living, breathing human beings, every day, in close proximity – human relationships are at the heart of schooling. What we do matters! Healthy relationships amongst all staff and students of the school are cultivated sometimes in the most basic of ways. In saying this, I am reminded of a student and a particular incident early on in my stay in the North.

Thirteen-year-old Eva had one of the sourest looks I have ever seen on a young person. A deep frown covered her face, a look of permanent anger. She smiled only in the presence of her very best friends and even those occasions were infrequent. I often felt she was looking at me from afar, out the corner of her eye, but she always turned her gaze away when I turned my attention towards her. Not being her teacher at the time, I only came into contact with her during breaks in the hallways or outside at recess.

One day, while on outdoor supervision, I absent mindedly walked past her and her friends sitting on the steps of a nearby portable. Eva waited for me to get right in front of her and then suddenly asked, "Why are you always smiling and in such a good mood?"

I answered, "Why not?" I paused then added, "I like smiling and I'm in a good mood most of the time."

Eva further inquired suspiciously, "But you can't always be in a good mood all of the time!"

"No ...," I agreed, "but if I do wake up in a bad mood, or if something really bugs me at school, why should I put everyone else in a bad mood? Besides, when I smile I feel better. Don't you?"

Eva did not answer – she just stared at me. Her friends had not entered into the conversation; they were quite content to watch and listen. I briefly considered prolonging our talk – this was the first time Eva had even given me the time of day. But I decided to continue on my rounds of the playground. As I left, Eva surprised me as her face lit up with the most genuine bright smile I could possibly imagine. "Okay! See you then!" she said, and I continued on my way. I couldn't help but chuckle to myself.

It seemed to me I had somehow passed a test. Eva still looked angry a lot of the time, but she smiled much more often than I had seen before that conversation. I have learned from many "Evas" that the connections we create in classrooms, in the school, and in the community are central to student development and growth as they try to figure out who they are and how they fit in their world. In learning alongside my students, I too have been able to negotiate my own educator identity along the way.

Respect, Respect and More Respect

I believe that educators must always remind themselves that we teach children, not subjects, and that every single person is deserving of respect and kindness. This makes sense to everyone, yet "walking the talk" sometimes proves difficult, especially in challenging circumstances. All teachers can recollect at least one particular student when pondering their times of difficulty over the years. Vanessa is one of those students for me.

Vanessa was an angry young junior high student. Her dark, piercing eyes and stern facial expression could bore holes into your very soul. I found it quite intimidating to face this young teen in my grade 8 science class. Although she was known to be very bright, I was cautioned by other teachers that Vanessa could act out with violent behaviour. She was also a natural leader and had the ability to draw other students into her disruptive ways. I was warned to not provoke her. The thing is, that despite her causing me to lose sleep at night, I liked her. I don't know why. There was just something genuinely redeeming about this girl. I figured I'd get to know her eventually. Being early in my career, I gingerly went about my job of teaching. Each day that I had to face that grade 8 science class, my stomach was in knots. *What would Vanessa do today?*

One day, late in October, Vanessa decided to have a tantrum, throwing a desk and chair across the room at a young boy. The other students were surprised, and quite nervous, immediately looking my way, awaiting my reaction. I paused for a moment, then directed Vanessa to step into the hall. I told her I would be out to see her shortly. Surprisingly, she went without any argument. I quickly organized some seatwork for the class, then went into the hall. Vanessa was waiting outside the door, bracing herself to be on the receiving end of yelling from an angry and frustrated teacher. She stared at me with what I assumed was tremendous dislike.

I can honestly say I had absolutely no idea of what I was going to say or do to this girl. I was not prepared for such a confrontation. I did know, however, that I had to deal with the situation – I couldn't ignore the behaviour. I did not say anything for what seemed like an eternity. We both stood in the hall, silently. I instinctively knew that raising my voice would accomplish nothing, never mind being extremely inappropriate from a cultural viewpoint. I still remember to this day the words that did eventually come.

"I know you are trying your absolute best to make me not like you, Vanessa." Long pause. Vanessa was motionless. "But it is too late – I decided I liked you a long time ago. No matter what you do I will still like you. You can't make me not like you, Vanessa."

As I slowly and calmly spoke these simple words, Vanessa's eyes filled with tears and she began to cry. I put my hand on her shoulder and steered her towards a hall chair near our classroom door. I told her that when she was ready, she was welcome to join the class and finish her work. I left her in the hall and returned to a hushed classroom. Two minutes later, as quiet as a lemming, Vanessa entered the room and continued on with her science work.

From that day on, Vanessa was an exemplary student in my class. I know that she was not an angel in all her classes, but for some reason I was able to say the right thing at the right time which allowed her to trust me. The next time Vanessa expressed anything that resembled anger towards me was three years later, after I had announced I would be leaving the community. It was after hours and we were both walking on the road near school. Vanessa looked at me and declared in her stern monotone voice, "You should stay until I graduate." That is all she said. She continued on with her friends. I knew what she was saying though, and I was touched by it. As it turned out, Vanessa became one of the youngest ever Baffin high school graduates exactly four years later.

I remember Vanessa with great affection. She taught me that all children need to be loved, no matter what. I learned that all students need to be given the benefit of the doubt. I learned that students with labels, who do sometimes behave badly, can change.

Children deserve to be respected. I learned as much from Vanessa as she did from me.

Throughout my life, I have found that when we treat others fairly, with respect and kindness, we are treated the same way in return. In schools, expectations of this sort need not be verbally expressed – they simply need to be modelled, understood and accepted.

I make an effort to understand where my students are "coming from." I remind myself each day that every child who walks through the doors of the school comes from a unique household with a unique history. Even the ones with challenging behaviours go home at the end of the day, hopefully, to loving parents and family. I feel that totally immersing myself in the cross-cultural environment of Inuit communities has allowed me to further develop the ability to see the world from another person's perspective. I try to walk in another person's *kamiks* every now and then so that I may begin to understand their personal point of view. Regularly adjusting and re-evaluating my own perspective as a teacher of Inuit students became absolutely critical throughout my years in Nunavut.

On Fairness and Discipline

Many teachers fall into the trap of believing that they have to treat every student equally in order to be fair. Yet if the aim in education is for an equality of outcomes for a wide range of students, then this simply cannot be true. Rather, we need to treat all students individually – which may mean *differently* – in order to be fair and equitable in our schools. This concept is confusing to many educators, so it is no surprise that even students themselves often misunderstand the meaning of "equal treatment."

Martha took longer to learn concepts than many of her peers. She often had to ask questions over and over again in order to understand even simple instructions. Martha wore thick glasses and leaned a little to one side as she walked. She frequently became impatient with herself and had difficulties controlling her outbursts of temper. One morning, during a science test, I could see evidence of her building frustration. By the end of the period, she was nowhere near completing the assessment. After her classmates had left for recess, I approached Martha and offered her the opportunity to come in after school to finish her test.

Her reaction was startling. "I don't want any special treatment!" she angrily replied as she quickly packed up her books and began to leave.

I had to think about my reply for a moment before continuing as I didn't want her to think that I was giving her "special treatment."

I said, "Martha, this is not special treatment. I do this for many students. I am interested in knowing what you know about science – I don't care how fast you can answer the questions. It is better for me to get an idea of what you have learned." Martha was not deterred. She was still heading for the door. I continued. "Sometimes I've given students an oral exam to test their knowledge. Sometimes I've asked students to take home a test and bring it back the next day. There are many ways that I can test you, Martha."

By now she was hesitating. She looked at me suspiciously. "I've never seen you do that. Who did you do that with?"

I told her that it didn't matter "who," but that everyone learns in different ways, and everyone reads and writes at their own speed.

Martha still objected. "But I'm not stupid. I don't want any special treatment."

I decided to let her think about it. I told her if she wanted, she could finish her test after school and reassured her she was not "getting something extra" that no one else ever got. I then quietly went about my way, organizing my desk for the next class. Martha left without another word.

Martha reminded me that students are keenly aware of your real or imagined perceptions of them. Martha wanted to be responsible for her learning in the same way as all of her peers – she needed to know I had the same high expectations for her as I did for everyone else. She needed to know I believed in her capabilities. She wanted to be measured against the same yardstick as everyone else. I believe it is crucial for all teachers to display high expectations for each of their students. Students will generally rise to that level. At the same time, however, teachers need to take individual needs and learning styles into consideration.

Martha did return to my classroom at the end of the day, in fine spirit, and finished her test. As she closed the door behind her, she smiled and said, "Thank you" before leaving.

Regarding discipline, I believe that school rules should be fair, reasonable, and applied consistently, but always taking into consideration the changing, individual circumstances of each and every child. I believe that good behaviour should be noticed much more often than bad behaviour. I adopted the strategy of "Catch them doing well, then praise them for it," an idea previously implemented in another Baffin school in the late 1980s. Joanne Tompkins felt that it served as a preventative approach to discipline. It is also a statement of how teachers value people in school. As a teacher, I heap positive encouragement on all of my students at any possible opportunity, even for small victories. Something deep within me recognizes that this simple acknowledgement is crucial to the development of a healthy self-esteem and personal confidence.

I believe in student-directed discipline. When students have a say in what is or is not acceptable school behaviour, as well as in the determining of the consequences for misbehaviours, students become true stakeholders in the system and they begin to police themselves, better than any one teacher could.

I have also seen the benefits of implementing alternative forms of behaviour management and discipline within the school setting, and involving students wherever possible. In one particular instance two young students in grade 7 were caught smoking on the school grounds. All students were aware that only the grade 9 to 12 students were allowed to smoke, and that if anyone broke the smoking rule, smoking privileges would be temporarily suspended for everyone.

The high school class was allowed to deal with the junior

smokers in a justice circle within the senior classroom. The older students sat in a large circle facing the offenders, who sat in the middle. I was pleasantly surprised to see there was no snickering or laughter. All students took their roles responsibly. Older students questioned the younger ones and discussion ensued to determine the appropriate "sentence" for the guilty parties. Students spoke Inuktitut, with Inuit staff looking on. The young students were quiet, looking down at their feet, visibly uncomfortable. For them, it would have been preferable to deal with the school principal. Being held accountable to their older sisters and brothers was much more difficult. The seniors deliberated for a long time but eventually decided on two days after-school detention and a promise to not break the rule again. Those two students did not find themselves in a justice circle a second time.

There is no place for put-downs or punishments in a warm, caring school environment. Empty threats have absolutely no place or value in school. It is important to deal with people in subtle, non-confrontational ways where possible. I am a very calm person in school. I take pride in the fact that I never, under any circumstances, raise my voice. I have learned over the years that calm, relaxed, firm tones, combined with periods of silent, patient waiting can accomplish much more than the excitable, impatient shouting that unfortunately occurs in many of today's classrooms. If a teacher truly believes in respecting all people, yelling at students is not a reflection of respectful treatment for all. I try to listen much more than I talk. Inuit have taught me the importance of waiting, and listening, and "speaking" without many words, and, perhaps above all, the power of silence.

Link to the Land

Inuit have always enjoyed a close relationship to the natural world. Inuit feel they *belong* to the land, as they have depended on it for survival and learned to adapt to its rhythms and cycles for centuries. To Inuit, "the land" includes all of nature – the earth itself, as well as the water, ice, wind, and sky, the plants and animals. *Inuuqatigiit* tells us that Inuit believe all living things are connected in a continuous cycle of life and cannot be separated.

One particular year, the ice was several weeks late in forming on the sea. Hunters were anxious to get out on the land. Their families missed the taste of country food, especially seal meat and *muktaq*, whale skin and blubber. As the days wore on, the tension in the community, and in the school, grew. At first, I didn't know why people were so edgy. Eventually I came to realize that the land for an Inuk represents a large part of his spiritual and emotional self. The act of going on the land to hunt or fish is not simply one of a need to eat – it is a much deeper need than anything physical. I have seen men and women completely renewed after even a short camping trip away from town. A feed of seal meat out on the ice with a companion may be all it takes to set a young man's, or woman's, mind right. My senior students were certainly affected in this way. Every now and then, one of them would approach me quietly and ask if they could go hunting instead of attending afternoon classes. I rarely denied them. How could I?

The monumental respect and deep caring for the animals on which Inuit depend was demonstrated to me one year, early in spring. A hunter discovered a large pod of beluga whales congregated at a small opening in the sea ice only a few hours from town. The news of the possibility of an easy and fruitful hunting opportunity so early in the season spread quickly. Snowmobiles and *qamouti* were packed up and groups of optimistic hunters headed out into the Sound in search of the whales.

For generations, Inuit hunters have followed the whales from one open area of the sea to another so that they could hunt the animals for food. When the hunters arrived, beluga whales by the tens were competing with each other for surface space in a small two by three metre opening in the frozen sea. Being marine mammals, these white whales require periodic visits to the surface so they can take in deep breaths of fresh air to replenish depleted oxygen supplies before diving back down to the ocean's depths. As it turned out, there were a handful of similarly sized breathing holes exposed throughout that region of the Sound. At each of these holes, five or six belugas at a time took turns surfacing for air before quickly submerging again.

These whales were in trouble. Such a large number of whales congregated in a small number of holes is unusual. The hunters concluded that other breathing holes in the immediate area must have closed up suddenly with the movement of the ice, leaving hundreds of these animals dependent on just a few cracks in the frozen sea. The belugas were in danger of drowning. As each whale reached the surface, a heavy burst of air could be heard, accompanied by a fountain of millions of water droplets expelled through its blowhole. As the animal began its return dive, the white dorsal surface of its body became visible for a moment. Deep gashes in the skin, from the bulbous head, over the blowhole, and down towards the tail, were evidence of the jagged ice surface at the edges of the breathing holes. Marauding polar bears on the ice near the site intimated a more gruesome story – many of the wounds inflicted on the whales were the result of bears clawing at them in the moments as they gasped for air. Several whales had severely torn blowholes. One was missing an eye.

Over the span of two or three days, nearly everyone in town made the pilgrimage over the ice to witness the plight of the trapped beluga whales. Canvas tents were erected on site by those who intended to stay longer than a day. Many students missed school that week. Instead, they were schooled in the real-life experience of witnessing an incredible natural phenomenon. Each day, those of us in town received updated news reports regarding the activities out on the Sound.

Members of the Hunters and Trappers Organization and the Renewable Resource Officer carefully monitored the situation, and after countless hours of consulting with community hunters and Elders they decided that ten to fifteen whales could be shot and harvested for food. Only the most severely injured would be taken. A sudden and drastic decline in the beluga population now would greatly affect their hunting quotas in the seasons to come. Inuit wanted to ensure that the population remain healthy and that subsequent hunting seasons would also be fruitful.

As each beluga was shot dead, a harpoon was immediately lanced into the animal. The head of the razor-sharp harpoon cut deep into the tissues of the whale. Groups of Inuit pulled with all their might on the rope attached to the head of the harpoon. As grave a situation as it was, they did not waste the opportunity to teach and learn from the event. Men, women, teenagers, and young children joined in on the action. Everyone shared in the experience. As soon as each whale was hauled up and out of the water, then dragged onto the ice, three or four people would immediately start to butcher the animal. Everyone in town, YoAnne and I included, received their share of *muktaq* that spring.

A decision was made to drill as many holes in the ice as was necessary to provide the whales with additional breathing holes. The holes would be drilled, one after another, in a line leading towards the open water at the floe edge several kilometres away. Every gas-powered auger in town was gathered for the job. Instead of participating in spring camp that year, two of my senior students, Russell and Manasie, opted to help Seeglook and the other men with the drilling. A third student wanted to help but found he could not – he was so greatly disturbed by the anguish of the whales that he returned to town. Eventually, after ten days of community help, most of the whales made it to safety.

I will never completely know what the land means to the Inuit psyche, truly, but my own upbringing allows for me to have a basic understanding. Living with Inuit, I learned to appreciate, in a deeper sense than ever before, the healing power of the land and of the therapeutic nature of an emotional and spiritual attachment to the earth.

Emotion

No one prepared me for the depth of emotion in teaching. Even now, after thirty years, it still surprises me every now and then. The fact that *love* enters into the everyday complexities of teaching is rarely mentioned in teacher education programs. Rather, educators are led to understand that in order to teach well, they must emotionally distance themselves from their students. Doing so is considered professional. I ask, *How is this truly possible?*

Educators come from many perspectives, experiences, and academic areas, but they all care about teaching and learning. They must also care about themselves, their colleagues, students, and communities. Earlier I mentioned that the teachers I most fondly remember from my own schooling are the ones who had an impact on my emotional well-being. I remember how they made me feel more so than what they were trying to teach me. Doesn't it make sense that students learn more when they know they are sincerely cared for by their teachers?

Even as a principal I cannot count the number of times that I choked back a lump in my throat or was brought to the verge of tears as I listened and spoke with a student in my office. Throughout the course of a week I would invariably have to intervene in a behavioural problem of some sort that needed to be addressed. After slowly gathering as much information as I could, I would usually ask the young girl or boy in front of me, "Would your mother and father be proud of what you have done?"

Not one student could ever answer this question aloud. Soon after the question was posed, tears would begin to well up in their eyes. I would give them time to think in silence. I would then remind them they were loved and supported by their family and they would still be loved regardless of their behaviours. I would hasten to add they were capable of much better things. Without exception I would tell students that the teachers, including myself, also cared about them in our own way, and that we were proud of having them in our school. By this time, I would be fighting the lump in my own throat. I would ask students to think about their actions before coming to school the next day and let them go.

This method of "soft" discipline proved quite effective for me. I truly believe that students want to do well and want to fit in, but they need to feel loved most of all. Joanne Tompkins said it best: Teachers and principals have to care enough to have faith that people will succeed and patience enough to support them when they stumble or are unsure.

The warmth of friendship that I encountered not only as a teacher but as a member of the community was humbling. I felt part of the community. I would never be Inuk and I would always be from away but I was accepted and welcomed. I was not expecting this. YoAnne too felt this same acceptance and sense of being welcomed. Early on in our stay in Grise Fiord, YoAnne's father passed away after a quick illness in December of that first year. She was not able to attend the funeral in Quebec, thousands of kilometres to the south. Without hesitation, the church Elders organized a memorial service for YoAnne's father. Hymns were sung and words were spoken – all in Inuktitut. It didn't matter. YoAnne and I were comforted. I brought photographs of Marcel to the church and they were passed from one person to another in the congregation. The community allowed YoAnne to grieve, and they grieved with her.

A month or so later, a new baby was born to one of my senior students. We heard that Susie and her family honoured Yo-Anne's father by adding his name to the considerable long line of names bestowed upon the newborn. This is an Inuit custom that has gone on for generations – Elders are remembered and honoured in this special way in all Inuit communities. We were both overwhelmed with the depth of the community's understanding of our loss and with the sincerity of their emotional support that we were forever changed by the experience.

I have alluded to the need for a warm and caring school environment. I have also expressed my belief that schools should reflect community. Individuals and families love and support one another; therefore, it follows that people in schools should love and support one another as well. I fully agree with Paulo Freire, the Brazilian philosopher, in that education is radically about love.

Educational Practise

I learned many things about good pedagogy, or educational practise, throughout my time in the Arctic. I believe in teaching the whole child, in offering a holistic education where academic needs are provided for as well as social, emotional, spiritual, and physical needs. I believe that content is not nearly as important as the process of learning, and that education should be relevant to the student's everyday life experience. To me, schooling should always take place within the cultural context of each and every child. I believe that education should be hands-on and activity-based. I believe in theme-based teaching that provides authentic experiences for students and incorporates a meaningful interdisciplinary approach to their schooling.

I believe in developing a respectful and caring school environment in which students can interact and teach others in formal and informal ways. I see peer tutoring as a valid, even essential, way to enhance student learning and social skills. Learning is social. I believe in co-operative learning and in the use of multiage groupings within the classroom. Again, this reflects real family and community life. Where possible, students should be encouraged to direct their own learning. Most importantly, every student should experience success as early and often as possible.

I have difficulty with the concept of grade designations. I would like to see students move along their individual continuum of learning at their own pace, in their own time. John Dewey, the educational philosopher, said it best: "Accept the child where the child is." As teachers, we then take that child and help lead him forward. I see the division system used in public schools as artificial. In a sense, we use grade designations as labels for students that force us to focus on the learning that is lacking instead of the successes achieved by the individuals. Why could high school students not simply count credits towards graduation, and forget about whether they are in grade 10, 11, or 12? And does it really matter how long it takes to attain that diploma? Why do we rush students through school? Every person is unique – so is their time frame for learning.

If programs are individualized for students, then it is not necessary to always place them in same ability groupings. In fact, mixed ability groups of students are a logical reflection of what occurs naturally within their community – older children often play with and care for younger children. Mixed age groups can learn from each other in more realistic settings. Family groupings in school allow children of various ages and abilities to interact with each other and foster an understanding that everyone is good at something, everyone needs help sometime, and all people can teach something to someone else.

* * *

So "am I ruined" as a teacher? The short answer, thankfully, is "no."

I know there are many schools in many communities throughout the world where holistic educational settings, which are humanistic and student-centred, aim to meet the individual needs of students. There are many educators who celebrate the diversity of students' cultures and languages in their classrooms. There are many educators who genuinely care, in a deep sense, for their students and schools. There are many educators who believe that learning should be joyful. And many teachers understand that we learn while we teach.

Even in situations where schools, districts, and boards seem oppressive to both students and teachers, individual educators can make profound differences in the lives of their students. Educators have choices in their approach to student culture and language. They have choices in the way in which they encourage parent and community involvement. They have choices in the way they assess students and implement teaching methodologies.

I will admit, however, that all of my teaching experiences from the moment I left Grise Fiord were, and still are, measured against those that I gained in the North. That experience is a difficult act to follow. Both YoAnne and I loved the work and we loved the life. We felt as if we were making a difference, somehow. Even now, twenty years since returning to Atlantic Canada, I view my time in the Arctic as very special – incomparable really, to any other work I have done.

YoAnne and I both lived deeply satisfying lives in

Pangnirtung, Hall Beach, and Grise Fiord. While our professional lives certainly evolved, our personal outlooks on life in general
were greatly enriched. We learned so much from our Inuit friends.
On a personal note, I learned how to be comfortable in silence
and to not always need to fill it with unnecessary chatter – I grew
to cherish more quiet moments, even in the presence of others.
I learned how to listen well and how to be far more patient. I
learned to not worry so much about time, and to have confidence
that the important things would get done, eventually. I learned
more about respect and not judging others. I learned the value of
not bringing too much attention to myself.

Living in the cross-cultural environment of the Inuit in
Nunavut, where land-based, traditional activities are still greatly
valued has only strengthened my convictions regarding culturally
relevant, holistic, and experiential education. My relationships with
Inuit, young and old, whom I have met along my journey, have
allowed me to be much more critical of my actions as an educator
in a diverse society. I am humbled and I thank all of them for this
incredible gift.

Epilogue

YoAnne and I left Grise Fiord in June of 1999, two months after
the official birth of the new Nunavut Territory. We celebrated the
new territory for the months and weeks leading up to April 1, and
then in the community and on the sea ice that very day, with every
single other resident of Grise Fiord. A group of young school children sang a song, followed by a prayer by Aksakjuk, an *aya* song
and drum dancer, then the raising of the brand-new Nunavut flag
in front of the RCMP trailer. Games were played for hours on the
ice, followed by a community feast in the gymnasium.

In the past twenty years many changes that we are unaware
of have occurred in the villages in which we lived and worked.
For one thing, all communities now have full access to the Internet and social media – we can even watch drone footage of Grise
Fiord on YouTube. Times have changed indeed! We have kept in
touch with a few Inuit, more so now than in the first decade after
moving back "south." Now that Facebook and MSN have made it all
the way north to Ellesmere Island, we hear random tidbits of information about our former home in Grise. We see there are many
more personal vehicles being driven in town. Many of our former
students drive their own trucks, brought to them on the annual
sealift. There is a new church, replacing the one that burned several years ago. There are now twice weekly flights into Grise Fiord

from Resolute Bay. There is an airport building where people can get out of the cold while waiting for the Twin Otter to arrive or depart.

Of my senior students, Jeffrey, became the fire chief for a while – he still lives there with Susie and their expanding family; Manasie and Susie, too, remain in Grise Fiord with their growing brood. Russell became an RCMP officer for a few years, and now works in resource conservation. He lives with his new family in Kuglugtuk. PJ, the junior high student who broke his leg, went on to become the twice-elected (so far) president of the Qikiqtani Inuit Association, a not-for-profit society which represents approximately 14,000 Inuit in the Qikiqtani (Baffin) Region of Nunavut. Carol was one of my students; her husband, David, is the Deputy Premier of Nunavut, and has held numerous portfolios as a member of the legislative assembly. These are just a handful we happen to know a little about.

The education system in Canada's newest territory has had its ups and downs. The 1993 Nunavut Land Claims Agreement that led to the creation of the new territory in 1999 did not include any stipulations about the education system for Inuit, and unfortunately there was no direct federal funding made available. However, a 2007 landmark document, *Inuit Qaujimajatuqangit: Education Framework for Nunavut Curriculum*, articulated a new vision of Inuit education. *Inuit Qaujimajatuqangit* (IQ) refers to the worldview, beliefs, principles, values, laws, skills, knowledge, and attitudes of Inuit. This document is now the source of all policy, curriculum, and programming carried out by the Nunavut government. Educators in Nunavut are expected to understand IQ, how it affects curriculum, and what this means for the practise of learning and teaching in Nunavut schools; IQ also offers a source of Inuit Elder knowledge and an application of that knowledge to the context of schooling.

In 2008, the new Nunavut Education Act became the first provincial or territorial education legislation in Canada to represent the educational vision of an Indigenous population. The Act states that it is the responsibility of the Minister, the district education authorities, and the education staff to ensure that Inuit societal values and the principles and concepts of IQ are incorporated throughout, and fostered by, the public education system. Inuit are patient people. I know that the people of Nunavut will continue to find their way. They already have a great start.

I would like to say that many of the pedagogical philosophies and strategies for teaching in Nunavut throughout our time there were light-years ahead of many that I observed being practised in southern educational institutions upon our return south. How easy it is for southerners to assume that teaching in the North would be "old fashioned," primitive even! Educators teaching within the Baffin Divisional Board of Education were simply asked to respect and incorporate Inuit language, culture, and knowledge into the daily routines of school and then they were given the freedom to figure it out and innovate away, one day at a time. Challenging? Yes! Impossible? No! The fact is, we did not realize how progressive we were at the time.

I was surprised to learn that there are fewer people living in Grise Fiord in 2019, approximately 130, and many fewer students in the school, about 35. Whereas most Nunavut communities are growing, its most remote community is not. Sadly, young Inuit in Grise today are more likely to leave the community for a life and work elsewhere. In a 2011 government sustainability report, residents of Grise Fiord suggested that improved infrastructure (a larger school and a community arena, for example) was needed to ensure that students who leave for higher education or work would eventually return home. They felt that the hamlet needed to be a more attractive and healthier place in which to live so that students would return and professionals would choose to work there.

YoAnne and I were two professionals who chose to live and work in Grise Fiord way back in 1995. We loved every minute of the experience. We never once thought of Grise as anything other than a magnificent place. We always felt privileged to be there. We have no doubt that today Grise Fiord is still a strong, resilient community. We are confident that the fine people of Grise Fiord will continue to make the hamlet that very unique and special place.

Acknowledgements

First and foremost, I thank YoAnne, my partner and constant companion over the past thirty-six years. Everything I have accomplished was made sweeter, more exciting, and more meaningful because it was shared with this amazing woman. We travelled north together and experienced a decade of living and teaching in extraordinary circumstances. We experienced the awe and wonder of the land and its people in one another's company. We shared in all of the successes and challenges I speak of within the pages of this memoir. We laughed and cried; we encouraged each another in difficult times. YoAnne's continued support of my new writing life over the past few years is greatly appreciated – her contribution to this particular story immeasurable.

I am in debt to all of the Inuit, young and old, who I have had the privilege to meet. The kindness and warmth of friendship that I experienced from so many people along the way is truly remarkable. I learned so much from many individuals. I thank the Elders (many of whom have since passed away) who helped me understand their world through their wisdom and unique perspective – Rynee, Abraham, Annie, Tookilkee, Martha, Geela, and Aksayook in particular.

I benefited from the insights of countless others over the years. Thank you to Larry, Annie, Seeglook, Jaypetee, Anne, and Meeka. I owe much to my teaching colleagues from all three of the communities in which we lived, including Mary, Mimi, Jane, Harry, Goretti, Monica, Martha, Lena, Ishmael, Leah, Wendy, Michael, and Anneke; I am in debt to them all for making my job that much easier.

Although I would like to, I cannot possibly name all of my students in the North. Yet they are the reason I stayed in the Arctic as long as I did. Each and every one of them contributed to my understanding of what teaching and learning is all about.

In my professional career as an educator in the Arctic, much support was provided by the local District Education Authorities and the then Baffin Divisional Education Council. Special thanks to Larry, Liza, Marty, Fiona, Greg, Steve, and Cathy.

Fiona and Anne-Louise both helped me find my voice in the early writing of this story as I completed my thesis for a Master of Education degree at the University of Prince Edward Island.

In my more recent involvement with the world of writing, I have found great support and encouragement from new writer friends – Colleen, Beth, and Kate, especially – and a whole new community at the Writers' Federation of New Brunswick. Thanks to Marjorie Simmins for her wonderful memoir workshop in Pugwash, Nova Scotia. Thanks also to Lesley Choyce at Pottersfield Press for taking an interest in my story at the Pitch the Publisher panel at Word on the Street (Halifax). And thank you, Cindy, for typing up my first draft.

Last but not least, I thank my parents for a wonderful upbringing and for the opportunities they provided for me in my life. At no time ever did they tell me I could not try something I really wanted to do. Without their love and confidence in my abilities, I would not have been able to live the life I feel I have been so privileged to lead. Thanks, Mum and Dad ... the adventure continues!

Bibliography

Ashton-Warner, S. (1963). *Teacher*. Simon & Schuster, New York.

Baffin Divisional Board of Education. (1996). *Our future is now: Implementing Inuuqatigiit*. Baffin Divisional Board of Education, Iqaluit, NU.

Baffin Divisional Board of Education. (1998). *Piniaqtavut: Integrated program*. Baffin Divisional Board of Education, Iqaluit, NU.

Barth, R. (1990). *Improving schools from within*. Jossey-Bass, San Francisco, CA.

Blodgett, J. (1979). The historic period in Canadian Eskimo art. In Alma Houston (Ed.), *Inuit art: An anthology*. Watson & Dwyer, Winnipeg. 1988.

Connolly, F.M. & Clandinnin, D.J. (1988). *Teachers as curriculum planners*. Teachers College Press, New York.

Cummins, J. (1996). Negotiating identities: Education for empowerment in a diverse society. California Association for Bilingual Education, Ontario, CA.

Edwards, B. (1989). *Drawing on the right side of the brain*. (Rev. ed.). Jeremy P. Tarcher, Inc. Los Angeles, CA.

Eisner, E. (1999). Does experience in the arts boost academic achievement? *Art Education,* 51 (1), 7-15.

Gardner, H. (1993). *Multiple intelligences: the theory in practise.* Basic Books, New York.

Government of the Northwest Territories: Department of Economic Development (1996). Turning Traditions into Thriving Ventures. In: *NWT Community Digest.* 1996.

Government of Northwest Territories: Department of Education. (1991). *Our students our future: An educational framework.* YK.

Government of the Northwest Territories: Department of Education (1994). *People: Our focus for the future. A strategy for 2010.* YK.

Government of the Northwest Territories: Department of Education. (1996). *Inuuqatigiit: The curriculum from the Inuit perspective.* YK.

Government of the Northwest Territories: Department of Education. (1997). *People: Our focus for the future. A strategy for 2010. A report on progress.* YK.

Government of the Northwest Territories: Department of Education. (1999). *Towards excellence: A report on education in the NWT.* YK.

Government of Nunavut (2011). *Infrastructure for a sustainable Grise Fiord.* YK.

Kirkness, V.J. (1988). The power of language in determining success. *TESL Manitoba Journal 5,* 1-7.

McGhee, R. (1996). *Ancient people of the Arctic.* UBC Press, Vancouver, BC.

McGregor, H.E. (2011) *Inuit Education and Schools in the Eastern Arctic.* UBC Press, Vancouver, BC.

McGregor, H.E. (2012) Nunavut's Education Act: Education, Legislation, and Change in the Arctic. *The Northern Review*, 36 (Fall), 27-52.

McIntyre, D.J. & O'Hair, M.J. (1996). *The reflective roles of the classroom teacher*. Wadsworth, Belmont, CA.

McLaughlin, M.W. (2001). Community counts. *Educational Leadership, 58* (7), 14-18.

Moore, A.J. (2000). *Ways of learning, learning styles, and First Nations students: A teacher resource*. UBC Press, Vancouver, BC.

Nunavut Boards of Education. (1995). *Pauqatigiit: Professional needs of Nunavut educators – Analysis and possibilities.* Iqaluit, NWT.

O'Donoghue, F. (1998). *The hunger for professional learning in Nunavut schools*. Unpublished doctoral thesis. University of Toronto. ON.

Qikiqtani Inuit Association (2013). Qikiqtani Truth Commission, Community Histories 1950-1975. Inhabit Media Inc. (Iqaluit).

Qikiqtani Inuit Association (2013). Qikiqtani Truth Commission, Thematic Reports and Special Studies 1950-1975. Inhabit Media Inc. (Iqaluit).

Qikiqtani Inuit Association (2013). Qikiqtani Truth Commission, Thematic Reports and Special Studies 1950-1975, QTC Final Report: Achieving Saimaqatigiingniq. Inhabit Media Inc. (Iqaluit).

Skutnabb-Kangas, T., Phillipson, R., & Dunbar, R. (2019). *Is Nunavut Education Criminally Inadequate? An Analysis of Current Policies for Inuktut and English in Education, International and National Law, Linguistic and Cultural Genocide and Crimes Against Humanity*. Nunavut Tunngavik Incorporated, Iqaluit, NU.

Tompkins, J. (1998). *Teaching in a cold and windy place: Change in an Inuit school.* University of Toronto Press. Toronto, ON.

Tupman, D. (1999). Recapturing soul and spirit in arts education: Towards a Canadian vision. In: *Leadership, advocacy, communication: A vision for arts education in Canada.* Selected papers from the National Symposium on Arts Education, Victoria '98. B. Hanley, ed. Canadian Music Educators Association.

Wink, J. (2000). *Critical pedagogy: Notes from the real world.* (2nd ed.). Addison-Wesley Longman, Inc. New York, NY, and Don Mills, ON.